Our

Has Arrived

BY
ELIJAH MUHAMMAD
Messenger of Allah,
Leader and Teacher
to The American So-called Negro

Published by
Secretarius MEMPS Publications
111 E Dunlap Ave, Ste 1-217
Phoenix, AZ 85020-7802
Phone/Fax 602-466-7347
Email: secmemps@gmail.com
Web: www.memps.com

OTHER BOOKS BY ELIJAH MUHAMMAD

MESSAGE TO THE BLACK MAN IN AMERICA
HOW TO EAT TO LIVE
HOW TO EAT TO LIVE, PART TWO
THE FALL OF AMERICA

ISBN-13: 978-1884855740
ISBN-10: 1884855741

© 1974 by
ELIJAH MUHAMMAD
CHICAGO, ILLINOIS

PRINTED IN THE UNITED STATES OF AMERICA

II

Acknowledgement

In the name of Almighty Allah, Our Most Merciful Saviour, Our Deliverer, Who came in the Person of Master Fard Muhammad, Master of the Day of Judgment. To Allah alone do I submit and seek refuge.

In this book I have gathered Truth God gave to me and the way He gave it to me. The way He gave it to me was a flowing spring or a flowing fountain.

The Supreme Wisdom that I teach is what Allah has taught me. That Wisdom is called the Supreme Wisdom which is the Supreme Wisdom. I am equipped with the truth from Almighty God, Allah. No man on earth can teach you what I am teaching you. I am charged with the delivery of the message.

I thank Allah that I have been sent by Him. He is backing me up to bring the enemy to his well brought doom (hell). We want what God has taught us.

If I have 40 million helpers, they are helping; but they are not responsible for the message. I am the only one God will hold responsible for you not getting the Truth.

Assisting me in preparing this book were my staff of secretaries, especially Sister Valora Najieb; typesetting and composing staff directed by Brother Gene X Walton; my son, Herbert Muhammad who helped preserve my speeches and articles and who suggested compiling this book; Miss Yolande T. Robbins helped read proofs; Brother Eugene Majied and his Art staff; and Brother John Ali who coordinated the work of these who have been mentioned and the many others who contributed their effort helping to make this book possible. Thanks. Thanks. Thanks. I Thank Allah for their assistance and pray the peace and blessings of Allah be upon them.

Elijah Muhammad,
Messenger of Allah

CONTENTS

CONTENTS

VI

CHAPTER 1

The Black Man Must Know the Truth

No. 1 — To know the truth of the Presence of the God of Truth and that His presence is the Salvation of the Lost and Found people of America is to know your life and its happiness.

No. 2 — Truth is in favor of you and me; for the truth of our enemies whom we have been serving here in the U.S.A. for over 400 years (whom we did not know to be our enemies by nature) is the truth that the Black Man must have knowledge of to be able to keep from falling into the deceiving traps that are being laid by our enemies to catch us in their way which is opposed to the way of righteous of whom we are members.

No. 3 — The archdeceiver. We are warned throughout the Bible and Holy Qur'an to shun this deceiver if we are members of the Black Nation (the righteous). There is nothing that is left of the truth of these people that God has not made manifest. And I am teaching you daily of this people. There are some Black Americans who will, after knowledge, sympathize with the archdeceiver (the devil) for the sake of advantage. Even some of our highly educated people will accept speaking in defense of this arch enemy of ours for the sake of trying to gain higher places with the archdeceiver. And some of them will tell me and the believers of Islam that they do not believe in any religion nor in any God of religion. The Bible foretold that this kind of talk against the truth would come in the last days; that the fool will say in his heart "there is no God." This prophecy is now being fulfilled among even our most educated class of people.

You cannot see the hereafter unless you believe in righteousness and unless you are a submissive one to the God and Author of righteousness because righteousness is the type of world that we will have to live under after the destruction of this evil and deceitful world.

No. 4 — The Christian church. There are "die hards" in the Christian church. Slowly but surely the Spirit of Allah is making manifest to the Black Man that the church and its religion called Christianity is the chain that binds the Black Man in mental slavery (seeking salvation where there is none) and thinking that he must die first to get to heaven. This is really a misunderstanding because heaven is a condition of life and not a special place. Heaven is enjoying peace of mind and contentment with the God of the righteous and the Nation of the righteous. It can be here in America, in the isles of the Pacific, or on the continents of Asia and Africa. But it is only a condition of life.

Black Christian believers are warned in the Bible in the 18th Chapter of Revelation (last book) to come out of her ("her" means the way and belief of the white race and the so-called Christian religion) that we be not partakers with them in the Divine plagues of God upon her (U.S.A.). This is the religion that the prophets prophesied to you that the enemy will deceive you with. Christianity is not the teachings of Jesus. Their theologians and religious scientists will agree with us in a show-down that it was not the religion of Jesus; for the religion of Jesus was Islam as it was the religion of Moses and all the prophets of

2

God. The Holy Qur'an teaches us that the prophets' religion was none other than Islam, the religion of Truth, Freedom, Justice, and Equality. This, the Christians preach with their mouths, but they do not practice Truth, Freedom, Justice, and Equality with us, the Black people. Since knowledge of them, we do not want to follow them in any religion because they are not by nature made to lead people into righteousness.

No. 5—Revolution between white and Black is due to the work of Allah and His Truth among the Black people of America. Never before in all your life have you seen the white man so anxious to keep the Black man near to him in his society and especially in Christianity, the great false, deceiving religion. He even offers to bribe any Black people of note, but for accepting his invitation and high places, they are reduced by a sudden fall to the level of disgrace and shame.

No. 6 — Leaders. We, the Black Nation, today with the knowledge of the truth cannot accept leaders made and offered to us for our guidance. I warn each of you to no more accept the white man's made or chosen leaders for you. This is what has kept us bound in the mental chains of slavery since the days of slavery. Our leaders are by their choice. These kind of leaders are Uncle Toms who are licking the boots of the white man for his pleasure and wealth regardless of what happens to you and me; for they care not.

No. 7 — Abraham's prophecy. But, I ask you to remember this: in the parable in the Bible of the rich man and Lazarus — which means none other than the white and Black people of America — the rich man died deprived of authority and wealth. In the anguish of the torment of his loss of wealth and power, the

3

parable refers to the rich man as being in hell. And in this condition, the beggar (Lazarus) saw no hope in begging that once rich man any longer for some of his sumptuous food. Then he turned to go for self (Abraham's).

The prophecy which Abraham was the recipient of only means that after 400 years of our enslavement, all these things are coming to pass. I ask you to be in time and accept the truth and do not mix up the truth with falsehood while you know it for the sake of untrue friendship.

CHAPTER 2

The Sure Truth

(Taken from Chapter 69 of the Holy Qur'an). What is said there in Chapter 69 of the Holy Qur'an is so true and is being fulfilled in this day and time.

This Chapter is warning the people in the time of the Resurrection of the mentally dead of what happened in the histories of former people who were doomed to destruction and how they reacted to the truth and warning and how they called the truth of their approaching doom a lie. This Chapter is warning the people of the calamities that are now besetting America and Europe; the sure truth that they are heading for their doom like Ad and Thamud who gave the truth a lie and were overtaken by Allah's Judgment of a violent wind roaring seven days and eight nights. This was the kind of destruction that Allah destroyed them with.

The Chapter also mentions of the destruction of Sodom and Gomorrah — how these cities were overthrown by earthquakes and unto this day they have not been rebuilt.

Pharaoh who opposed the Truth and called it a lie suffered the Judgment of Allah (drowning in the Red Sea).

The Black Man in America is now suffering under the falsehood of his enemies while truth is being sounded in his ears. He sees the evidence of it with his eyes; yet he would like it a lie.

The main warning of the Holy Qur'an to those who take the truth for a lie and the lie for the truth is that

5

they are subject to the same type of Judgment that these former opponents of Allah were subjected to.

We are now witnessing the truth being spread all over the continent of America and jumping the borders and spreading around the earth. Allah is backing up His Coming and Presence to defend the horrible plight of the so-called American Negro.

There is no plainer truth that could ever come to both white and Black than what Allah, in the Person of Master Fard Muhammad to Whom praises are due forever, has delivered to me whom He chose to deliver this Message of Truth.

The enemy is ever seeking a way to oppose the truth and take you and me to their doom if we are foolish enough to give a lie to the truth.

Everything mentioned in the Bible and Holy Qur'an such as plagues and judgments taking place in ancient times of the Bible and Holy Qur'an against the opponents of Allah is to warn you and me that the same thing is coming upon America and Europe but America is No. 1 (first).

This is the truth that God has given to me to warn you. He (Allah) is Sufficient to back up His Own Words.

The cold and violent wind blowing for seven days and eight nights to destroy an enemy people of Allah; the earthquakes taking place, overthrowing cities; and the destruction of Pharoah and his army are to warn you and me that the same thing will take place here in America and is now going on (This is the sure truth).

The evidence of this sure truth that I, Elijah Muhammad, am preaching is that America is in for every known destruction that plagued the people of old.

As the Bible teaches us (symbolically), God says He will use every one of His arrows against the wicked world today. When a man says he will shoot all of his ammunition to try to kill you, you want to know how much ammunition he has to shoot. I say plenty, for Allah has no such thing as a limitation to what and how He can destroy since all the powers of heavens and earth are within His Hands.

The forces of nature (which He is using and will continue to use) are things that we have no defense against.

I say, Black Man, believe in Allah and come follow me.

CHAPTER 3

Knowledge of Time

If only the American so-called Negroes had knowledge of the time in which we now live, they would accept Islam at once; for it is just the acceptance of Islam which will bring the so-called Negroes the things they desire; good homes, money, and friendship in all walks of life. This is the time that they should enjoy such heaven — the Time of God. They are really chosen by God to be His people, and not the Jews nor white Christians. It is you, the American so-called Negro, but it is just you who are blind, deaf, and dumb to the knowledge of the Time of your salvation and the judgment and death of your enemies.

Remember the story of Moses and his people. Jehovah said to Moses: "I have surely seen the affliction of my people which are in Egypt, and I have heard their cry by reason of their taskmasters; for I know their sorrows" (Ex. 3:7). Jehovah had seen and heard the afflicitions and cries of His people while His people were yet dumb to the knowledge of Him, for they called not on Him. They worshipped the gods of Pharaoh and his people and not Jehovah Who was the God of their fathers. Jehovah had not represented Himself as being the God of Pharaoh and his people. It was to the slaves of Pharaoh and the slaves' fathers that Jehovah, their God, was to show mercy and deliverance.

Pharaoh was against Jehovah and His religion and the people of Jehovah who were his slaves. So it is and Allah's true religion of Islam. But it is time that the mentally dead Negroes, who are afflicted daily by the evil hand of white America, should be delivered and given freedom, justice, and equality and a land that they can call their own. Day and night their cries go up into the ear of Allah, the God of our people (the Muslims).

We cannot hope for justice from the devils when by nature there is none in them. All the day long the Negroes are mistreated. If Allah and I, His servant, will not stand up for them, who shall stand up for them? You, by far, are unable to do so; for you know not God. The devils have you afraid and worshipping that which you know not. Fear not and come follow me and God will love you and will set you in heaven at once while you live.

Jehovah told Moses to go first to the elders of Israel and say to them: "The Lord your God (not Pharaoh's) the God of your fathers, He has appeared unto me saying, "I have surely visited you and have seen that which is done unto you in Egypt (America)" (Ex. 3:16). But the elders would not even meet with Moses, only by way of disputation.

CHAPTER 4

The Hidden Truth

Hiding the truth is a very serious thing to do. It causes harm and disappointment and causes one to be misled. It causes loss of property and life. It causes the loss of friendship, beloved ones, and loss of confidence and trust.

In court, it causes heavy penalties and someone's being sent to prison or to death for that of which they are innocent.

The greatest and gravest of all is the slavemasters' hiding of the truth that will exalt and save his slave. This is that great truth that white America is hiding from her once - slaves (the Black man and woman). The white people know of and see the Salvation of their slaves that is now present. They are doing everything they possibly can to deceive the Black man and woman into thinking that they (white people) hold out greater and better promises for a future to the Black Man and woman in America than Allah (God). This will deceive many of our people. Read the 7th Surah (Chapter) of the Holy Qur'an where the devil is made to confess his deceiving of the people in these words: "Allah promised you the promise of truth. I promised you, but failed to fulfill."

As you know, the Revelation of the Bible under the title of John, teaches us that the old dragon beast (referring to the white civilization) deceived the whole world, and they have done just that. Allah has taught me they deceived 90 per cent of the total population of the planet earth. The only way the white race can survive and rule is by making false appear as truth and truth to appear as false.

The white race was made by nature without the truth. Jesus said (Bible John 8:44) that there was no truth in them, for their father was a liar and a murderer. Therefore his children (white race) cannot be otherwise.

We should know the truth of the seriousness of the time that we are now living in. The truth will save our lives if we believe it.

America is at war with the darker people (Brown, Yellow, and every race regardless of color) today, but she refuses to tell you the truth of this war that is now taking many lives.

This is hiding the truth. What is she trying to get peace for? If these people's losses are as great as the radio and other news media state, the enemy would be on his knees begging for peace. It seems as if it is now vice versa. This is hiding the truth.

Allah has said to me that America will not admit the truth of her losses until we see it on our heels. The Black Man of America never has put any confidence in anyone but his white slavemaster. Regardless of how ill - treated the Black Man may be, he still has hopes of his master telling him the truth.

The real truth is that America is under Divine Judgment to destroy her for the evils done to Allah's people (the Black Man in America).

Hiding the truth takes away confidence, trust, and love.

CHAPTER 5

Time

If you who disbelieve in the Truth would only consider the time in which we now live, you would bear witness that it is the very truth from your God that I am teaching. Just when should we expect Truth to be triumphant? The answer is: after the removal of falsehood.

The Time referred to in this book is the time of the present world as Allah (God) has revealed it. This time covers a period of six thousand years. It began from the day that the first white person was made which was in the year nine thousand of our calendar history.

This date is taken from the beginning of the present cycle of world history writings by 24 black scientists of which only 23 actually do the writing, and the 24th one acts as judge of the writings of the other 23. This takes place once every 25 thousand years. In this history is written everything that will come to pass for the next 25 thousand years.

The original scriptures of the Bible and Holy Qur'an were taken from it and revealed by word of mouth and inspiration to prophets. We are now in the 16th thousand year of this cycle and have nine thousand, nine hundred and fifty - six years to be finished before the next cycle. But we are only concerned with that which the present time holds for us. A thorough knowledge of the time and changes to be made is the important factor for you and me.

The time given to the white race (Yakub's grafted

people) to rule the world is between the ninth and fifteenth thousandth year of our cycle of 25 thousand years which is six thousand years.

This time expired in 1914. A few years of grace have been given to complete the resurrection of the Black man, and especially the so-called Negroes whom Allah has chosen for the change (a new nation and world). They (so-called Negroes) have been made so completely mentally dead by the enemy (white race) that the extra time is allowed.

The time (six thousand years) ruled by the white race has been the worst of our known history; a time of complete trouble-making, war, bloodshed, and death of both the righteous and the wicked as never before. Therefore, the black nation and our God, Who is the Originator of the universe, have decided to remove the troublemakers from our planet Earth, as there is no way of the black nations getting along in peace with this wicked, grafted race known as the white race. They have flooded the nations with deceit and divisions.

The time now has arrived for plain truth, wherein you shudder and call the truth a lie and call falsehood the truth.

This is due to your being reared and taught by the deceiver! But your disbelief in the truth will not hinder its progress, for it is the Time of Truth and this Truth is in our favor.

The white race progressed under falsehood for the past four thousand years because it was given to them.

Now, that time has expired and the time of truth and righteousness again will rule. The interval of six thousand years of evil and falsehood makes the average person think that the original black nation was never anything worthwhile. Consider the time!

Most surely man is in loss except those who believe and do good and enjoin on each other truth (Holy Qur'an) 103:1-3). The time of the white race is divided into three periods of two thousand years each.

The first two thousand years was the period between Yakub, the father and grafter of the white race, to the birth of Musa (Moses) to the birth of Isa (Jesus), the last Great Prophet to the white race. The third two thousand year period is from the birth of Isa (Jesus) to the coming of Allah, often referred to by the Christians as: "The coming of God, the Christ, the Messiah, the Son of Man", or the "second coming of Jesus." In Islam, it is referred to as the "Coming of the Great Madhi, the coming of Allah" to the birth of Muhammad.

CHAPTER 6

Truth

I am well aware of my disputers who dispute without knowledge and who are followers of the devils for certain privileges. They claim to be representatives of God and Jesus Whom they claim to be the Son of God, but they are licensed, ordained, and sent by the devils (God-sent men are licensed by the world). This class which loves to be revered and honored by the people whether God has any respect for them or not are really agents of the slavemasters (the devils). They are secret persecutors and murderers of the prophets of God and will say: "If they had been in the days of the prophets, they would have been their followers and would not have opposed them." Yet they persecute me and my followers and all who teach the truth for the same reason that the enemies did to the prophets of old.

It was special privileges that Pharaoh offered the "enchanters" to oppose Moses as being a liar. "He promised them that they would be drawn near to him," (Pharaoh); Holy Qur'an (7:113, 114). It is the nearness (friendship) of the white race that the majority of the so - called Negro preachers seek, and not the nearness, love, and friendship of God. They openly confess that in their position (licensed and missioned by the white race to preach according to their likings), they cannot preach the truth if that truth is against the white race. Their followers' (church members) burdens are ever made grievous to carry because of the love and fear of their enemies by

15

the preachers. They call preaching the truth hatred.

The source from which my teaching springs, or fountain from which I drink, is the same source from which Noah, Abraham, Moses, and Jesus drank — Almighty Allah (God) in whom you probably do not believe; as the disbelievers of the above - mentioned prophets did not believe in those prophets' truth.

The early man (original man) knew the earth's revolutions, the circulation of blood, and the existence of microbes. The only man or people who were late in acquiring such knowledge was the white race which is the only late or new race we have on our planet. "Adherence to the unknown is a throw-back to anyone or nation." This is the number one holdback to the so-called American Negro. Without the knowledge of self or anyone else, or the God of their salvation they are lost, strictly adhering to or following those who preach and represent a mystery God (unknown), but yet charge that mystery God with getting a son out of wedlock and of waiting 4,000 years to produce His Son to give His made people (the Adamic race) the religion called Christianity. This is the gravest charge that could be made against the all-wise, all-knowing, and all-powerful God. And they say: "The beneficent God has taken to Himself a Son." Certainly this is an abominable assertion; the heavens may almost be rent there at, and the earth cleave asunder, and the mountains fall down in pieces that they (the Christians' preachers) ascribe a Son to the beneficent God. And it is not worthy of the beneficent God that He should like to Himself a Son. "There is no one in the heavens and the earth, but will come to the beneficent God as a servant." Holy Qur'an (19:88-93).

I bear witness with the above-said; that an all-wise, all- powerful God does not need a Son; and if He

16

would get one as the Christians charge Him (out of wedlock), He could be charged with adultery. I repeat, "The white man's so-called Christianity is not only no good for the Black man; but it is fast proving to be no good for the white race who are the founders of that religion, and not Jesus, as they would like for you to believe."

CHAPTER 7

Time Has Arrived That Allah Will Fulfill His Promise

The so-called Negroes are the prey (Isa. 49:24) of the mighty United States as Israel was in the days of Pharaoh. They were a prey under the power of Pharaoh. According to the Bible, they had nothing like a share in the land of Egypt. A few cattle and the land or home given to Joseph's father house in the days of Joseph all seemed to have disappeared in the time of Moses.

Jehovah appeared to Moses in the bush. Moses was made to see the bush in a flame of fire though there was no actual fire. The fire represented the anger of Jehovah against Pharaoh and his people. It was a declaration of a divine war against the Egyptians for the deliverance of Israel.

The time has arrived that Allah (God) should fulfill His promise made to Abraham. According to the Bible (Gen. 15:13, 14) we do not find wherein Israel had ever sought Jehovah through prayer or from any scripture; nor did they know of any prophet before Moses. The only knowledge we have is in the words of Jehovah's address to Moses — that they knew Him only by the name of God Almighty (Ex. 6:3).

But the real issue was not in the name as much as it was in the time. It was the time that Jehovah should fulfill His promise, though Israel was a disbelieving people in Moses and Jehovah. Jehovah could not lie to His prophet, Abraham, though Israel was a rebellious people (disbelievers) and Pharaoh had to know the time of his end. There was a limit to his rule over the people of God, though they knew not their God nor their fathers. The time had arrived that they should be delivered from the power of Pharaoh, and that they should become an independent people in a land that they would be given that they could call their own.

The devils are universal snoopers. They pretend to be interested in your spiritual meetings, but only to listen to what you are saying among yourselves. You may see him in all of the churches and gathering places of the so - called Negroes listening in on their meetings to keep them from accepting the Truth (Islam). The so-called Negroes think that it is an honor to have the devils come among them because they are ignorant to this, their open enemies' intentions.

I am for the separation of my people from their enemies; that they share not in their enemies' destruction, even though I may lose my own life in this daring attempt to save them by the plain, simple Truth of God and Power. It must and will be done regardless of whom or what. It can be done in one day, but Allah desires to make Himself known in the West, as it is written of Him.

Our sixty-six trillion years from the moon have proven a great and wise show of the Original Power — to build wonders in the heavens and earth. Six thousand years ago, or to be more exact, 6,600 years ago, as Allah taught me, our nation gave birth to another god whose name was Yakub. He started studying the life germ of man to try and make a new creation (new man) which our twenty-four scientists had foretold eight thousand four hundred years before the birth of Mr. Yakub; and the scientists were aware of his birth, before he was born, as they are today of the intentions or ideas of the present world.

19

CHAPTER 8

Never Taught A True
Knowledge Of God

You, who have been here in America for four hundred years, have never been taught a true knowledge of self, God, and His religion, Islam. As long as you are without such essential knowledge, which is the key of salvation, freedom, justice, and equality, you are not free. It is true that the truth shall make the lost and found members of the Tribe of Shabazz (the so-called Negroes) free, (John 8:32) but they have never known what truth it was that shall make them free.

That truth comes to us at the end of the Caucasian world. The end has come and Allah has also come to make manifest this hidden truth to us, the Black nation of the earth; and first, to the lost members of that nation. According to the Bible and Holy Qur'an Sharrief, it is the divine purpose of Allah to make known this hidden truth that shall make the Black nation free.

A thorough knowledge of our own history and the history of the white race has been kept from the ears of the Black people of America who were enslaved by their enemies and the enemies of all dark people the world over.

The so-called Negroes' problem of getting the truth is very hard, but the hardest problem to solve is getting them to believe it after getting it in their ears. This is due to their being brought up solely under the teachings of their enemies.

Black people are schooled one hundred per cent in

the fear of their enemies and the enemies' own fixed religion called Christianity with the name of Prophet Jesus on it in order to make them believe that it came from Jesus. But their enemy's own translation of the Bible omitted the mentioning of any of the prophets' religions by name.

On the other hand, the Holy Qur'an teaches us that the prophets' religion was none other than Islam, the Religion of Peace.

Shall we accept the scholars of the white race to teach us the knowledge of our God and history which has no birth record while they themselves were made by one of our own gods only six thousand years ago?

Let us give praise for the coming of our God, Allah, Who came in the person of Master Fard Muhammad, and whom our enemies persecuted and ordered out of the country. His power they cannot persecute and drive out.

Neither persecution, evil spoken, nor death will stop this truth that shall make you free which I have received from the very mouth of Allah (God); for it is time that the dead (so-called Negroes) should know the truth and accept their own place among their own kind in the holy nation of Islam.

This is the time. There never will be any peace among the nations of earth until the so-called Negroes have heard the truth and those who accept it are separated and placed in the paradise of their God, Allah.

The so-called American Negroes, with their God, Allah, shall become the universal rulers, believe it or not. They can do it now if they will quit this slavery religion called Christianity. No Black people who accept Christianity will ever be free.

You automatically become the servant of the white

race and not of God upon accepting their religion. The so-called Negroes, with their leaders, should come out of it into their own religion; but they cannot until they first have a thorough knowledge of self and others.

CHAPTER 9

The Truth And Our Mistakes

"Oh Allah, Originator of the Heavens and the Earth, Knower of the seen and the unseen, Thou judgest between Thy servants as to that wherein they differ." (Holy Qur'an 39:46).

No civilized nation wants the so-called Negroes. Only Allah, our Loving and Most Merciful God Who came in the person of Master Fard Muhammad in 1930, will accept us. It was not until 1933 that he began revealing his true self to us as being the answer to the Prophecy of Jesus, the coming of the Son of Man, the Seeker of the Lost Sheep. (I was expecting Him. The devils knew acquaint the so-called Negroes with Him). They will never acquaint the so-called Negroes with Him, nor will they ever tell you anything of good that is in your favor. Even if all of their enemy nations were closing in on them, they would not tell you until you saw them.

I am not concerned with what the white race believes in as a religion. They are not my people nor are we their people nor is our God their God. I am never surprised to see or hear of evils committed by white people. The only time they would surprise me is on seeing or hearing of some good that they are doing.

My people, the so-called Negroes, will soon learn and recognize the Truth, for the Author of Truth is with us. They yell their lungs out over a dead Prophet (Jesus of two thousand years ago) who cannot and did not come to do anything for us but prophesy of us

23

going into slavery and of God delivering us; and He was not even sent to us. The white race and their tampering with the Truth of the Bible (their slave-making Christianity) have poisoned the very hearts of our people against themselves and their Own God. No one can unite the so-called Negroes in America without the help of Allah (God). We must think of self-unity, and not love and unity with our enemies whom Allah (God) will destroy from the face of the earth in the very near future.

In their minds they are saying to me that Allah (God) does not want our enemies. "We do not want Allah (God) nor His religion if our enemies are not accepted." Their ignorance make fools of themselves; they love their enemies in spite of the fact that the white slavemasters kept our fathers out of their religion, Christianity, for approximately three hundred years. As long as they were children, they accepted the fixed and poisoned white man's religion. Now today, the white slavemasters are scared stiff from looking at the consequence coming to them for their deceiving the world of the Black Nation. Now they sit with you in your church. They are not there to hear you preach and teach them of their own religion, but to **deceive** you into thinking that now we all are brothers and God's people together; and that the church is the place for your safety and that you should not believe in any other religion other than Christianity. They try to convince you that the church is Jesus' house where He has put His name and "the Gates of Hell shall not prevail against it." And remember what He said to Peter: "Upon this rock I build My church."

After the injection of such poison, the so-called Negroes are lulled off to sleep with the death of the ignorant; The Gates of Hell will not try prevailing against itself, but the "Gates of Heaven" are now prevailing against the church and all that she stands for. And the "Gates of Hell" will not prevail against the "Gates of Heaven" (Allah and Islam).

If Peter's confession was the only thing necessary for Jesus to build the church, he should have been able, with twelve disciples, to have converted all of the Jews and destroyed their temples with the stone of Peter. But he did not; for Jesus was not the Founder of the white man's religion and church any more than was Moses or the former Prophets of Allah (God).

The Bible further says that Jesus said to Peter, "Flesh and blood did not reveal it to him." We never get Divine Truth unless it comes through flesh and blood. But really the flesh and blood that will not reveal truth is the devil (white race). Such is fulfilled today.

CHAPTER 10

I Want To Teach You

Yesterday you could not find Me. I was so wrapped in the mist that people were trampling on me and they didn't know that I was down there in the mud. All praise is due to Allah. Allah Is all of us. But we have a Supreme One that we can throw this name 'Holy' upon. He Is Allah, The One over all of us; The Most Supreme One, the Wisest One, the Mightiest One; The One that Sees and Hears that which we can't see and hear. That Is He. He Is rooted in all of us. Every righteous person is a god. We are all God. When we say "Allah" we mean every righteous person. Allah teaches me that He is a man — not something that is other than man. The Holy Qur'an refers to Him in such pronouns as 'He' and as 'We and as 'Us.'

There are so many of us who are ready to argue and dispute about the God. If you don't believe that he is a man, then bring me the one that you represent.

You say, 'I don't believe in God being a man.' What do you believe in? Show me what you believe in. I can show you my God. Show me yours. On the Day of Resurrection, the Bible and the Holy Qur'an teach us that we will be brought face to face with The True God; the evil and the Good One. This is going on today, my friends. If I preach to you that the white race is the devil, then where is the Good God? If this is the evil god, then where is the Good One?

If you tell me that he doesn't have any form, then I say how in the world can you prove to me that you are making me acquainted with a God? How can I see nothing? Some enemies of the True God, the Visible

26

God, have deceived you and are making you think that there is no such thing as a visible god.

I want to say to you, my friends, if you don't have one that is visible — see Allah the visible way!

The Bible and the Qur'an teach me and you that on this day there is a man whom God Chose for His Last Messenger. Whom have you benefited by other than a man? Do you sit down and pray to the space in the sky to drop you down some wheat? You may look up that way, but the wheat comes out from under your feet. You don't plant wheat in the sky. You plant it in the earth and it comes up out of the earth. And the Holy Qur'an teaches us that we have root in the earth.

Everything that breathes is Allah's. Out of it (the earth) comes our bread and meat and out of it comes us. We come out of the earth. We don't drop down out of space. But all of us come up out of the earth. If we are born from some man and woman, they came from the earth. The very sperm that makes a human being appears out of water and out of the vegetation of the earth — it didn't drop out of space.

I want to teach you who you are. So many people have been made blind, deaf and dumb to the knowledge of God. Why are they made deaf and dumb to the knowledge of God? Because they are blind, deaf and dumb to the knowledge of self. How can they know God? But Allah Is here and Has Risen up in your midst by the Power and Wisdom of the Supreme Who is a Man to teach you the knowledge of self and the knowledge of God and the Devil.

Some people don't want you to teach them who the devil is because they love the devil. They don't want to bear with me that this is the devil. But the Holy Qur'an teaches you and me and the Bible also. They don't want it translated into their language but nevertheless they didn't get all of this out of our knowledge. They are visible people; they are not invisible people. They are visible and on the Last Day these true people will be made manifest to you and me. The devil will be made manifest to us as he is. The Holy Qur'an teaches that he is an open enemy. He is not something concealed; he is not something invisible. But he is a visible being.

Your Lord Is One Lord. If He were a spirit He couldn't be one spirit because there are many spirits. Can you believe that your God Is something that is not visible but yet He has great interest in man's affairs? Who other than a man will care about your affairs?

Take, for instance, the wild beasts — they don't care anything about you or me...except to try and stay out of our way!

Now here is something standing out here with no form at all...and on the Day of Resurrection we will see Him, but nevertheless He still will be invisible; He will be a spirit!

We should get away from that. We used to not believe that man could go to the moon. But if he goes to the moon, that shows you that he is god and not the moon and the flying apparatus that he made and went up there on. No one came down from the moon and taught him how to get up there. He was god enough in himself to fix up a machine that would take him to the moon. It was not an invisible god that taught him how to measure the distance. It was a visible God that taught him mathematics.

You may ask me, "Well why did we not know all of this?" Because you were under an enemy of yours who wanted to make you ignorant so he could move you and me. That is why you are in such condition that you are now; because he actually made you like this.

28

CHAPTER 11

The Knowledge of God Himself
(Saviour's Day, February 26, 1969)

We thank Allah for His great Blessings that He has bestowed upon us, to remember us, who were lost and now found, whom He Himself came forth, leaving everything of His Glory and coming to us. He came searching the Earth to find and locate that lost member of the Aboriginal people here in the farthest part of our planet, the West, who were brought here over 400 years ago in chains. There is One that has been born to take the shackles off us and relieve us of those chains that have shackled and poisoned us for 400 years. We are happy and thankful to that God; a God that has mercy on us; a God that loves us. We are happy and thankful to be here, to bear witness that today we have on our side a God who is able to lead and guide us and protect us and deliver us back to our own. We are happy.

Glory has many obstacles. We are tried by many things. We have a hard way getting back home, as we did leaving home. But we want to say to you that this is not Our Saviour's Day as we call it by birth, but it is Our Saviour's Day because every day is Our Saviour's Day!

For the first time since our fathers fell into the chains and shackles of their enemies and were brought here for the purpose of being made blind, deaf, and dumb, we have come to the knowledge of self, to the knowledge of our God, our people, and to the knowledge of the way back to our Native land. For the first time, a Friend has come to us! A Friend, indeed! A Friend who is so powerful that He can just desire a thing, or say, "Be" and it comes to pass. Such a Friend! I'd like to be His Friend!

But first we want to consider a few topics. We want to think over how it happens that we are here. We want to think over the time that we are now living in. "Why, Elijah Muhammad, are you always preaching all over the country that this is Judgment?" "Why, Elijah Muhammad, are you constantly warning us that we ought to unite with our own kind?" "What is going to happen to other than our kind?" "Why should we separate?" "Why should we unite to ourself and not to everybody?" "Why should we think more of ourself than we think of other people?" "Why should we leave the religion of other people and come to what you call Islam?" "Why should we serve another God?" "Why should we believe in another religion?" "Is not the religion called Christianity right for us?" "Why should we give up our Christian names?" "Are not the Christian names of the white people right for us?"

I only want to acquaint you with what belongs to you.

If you are free, why not exercise that freedom? You can't be free if you are begging and serving and looking forward to freedom from a master who says he freed you a hundred years ago. Let's look at these few little topics. You say, "I don't want to be separated." Who said that they are going to force you to separate?

Our fathers were brought here; not that they came of their own accord. They were brought here. They were forced to come here. They wanted to return home, but they could not swim 9,000 miles. They stood on the shore of North America with grief - tears flowing down their Black cheeks begging that "Ship," "Oh, Ship Jesus, take me back," But it was leaving them. They knew not the people! Oh, I want us just to look into this thing. They knew not the strangers because it had been prophesied and predicted a long time ago to Abraham that they would dwell among strangers, not among their acquaintance, but among strangers and in a strange land. Think that over, Brothers. In a strange land they will dwell. "But after 400 years, I will judge that people." "And bring again, Abraham, your people." Who is Abraham? The Holy Qur'an, the 22nd Surah, says that Abraham gave us the name of Muslims. Who gives you Christianity? Who gives you Christian names? We want to look into it a little. You say your name is that which white people call themselves by. Are you white people? You say, "Christianity is my religion; it's Jesus' religion." Who said it was Jesus' religion? Did Jesus say that it was his religion? You are now arguing, fighting, and disputing over the religion in which you should believe, having no knowledge of your own religion nor the one that you are in that is not yours.

How can Christianity be God's Religion? How can it be His Religion when He changes not? Did He give that religion to Adam? No. The Adam - people, from the time of Moses to the time of Muhammad, had their own religion, their own God. We know by their history. Every nation on the earth has its own God, and still has its own God, but you. You bow down and worship what your slavemaster says to worship, and that He is a Mystery. That means I don't know Him. A Mystery God is One that no one knows. I think the white man is pretty smart. He puts you in falsehood and fixes it so that you cannot condemn him. You ask

31

him, "Where is that God?" He says, "Look up." "Where is that heaven?" He says, "Look up." I say he is a very smart man to fool people by the hundreds and millions and whole nations and races. They don't question. They bow their heads and say, "Yes sir." — and go on with nothing. Say, where is that God? No man knows. He doesn't even think to ask, "Well what are you trying to teach me then?" He never asks any questions — takes, it and swallows it, hook, line, and sinker. No questions. Then you come and say: "Look, I have a little statue over here, I have a God! Oh, you should bow." What do you worship, Mister? "I worship God." "Well, where is He?" "Oh, no man has ever seen Him." And if no man has ever seen God at any time, then no man knows anything about the God.

Well, you and I will come to some conclusion about this thing in a while. Hindus have been on this planet for untold ages. They are an Original people. They have been here for a long, long time. For 35,000 years, they have been worshipping other than the Real God. Think that over. But that's no time. After a while we will learn that that is nothing; just 35 days or 35 minutes to time. A long, long time! We are talking about Gods today. I want you to have patience. God let the Hindu go astray and worship whatever he wants to. Today you find the Hindu with more gods than he can mention. Everything is a god to the Hindu. He is far worse than any religious people you know of. He makes his God, and when he gets out of ideas how to make them, he starts worshipping himself. That's the Hindu. God was talking with me about these two people, the Christian and the Hindu, one day. He said, "You know, Brother," (He called me 'Brother.') He said, "There is a law among Us, a ruling;" He said, "if the Hindu and the Christian are walking together," He said, "kill the Hindu first because the Hindu is

32

more poison than the Christian." And he is. For 35,000 years he has been believing in other than the Real God; that's a long time; 29,000 years before the Christians.

We have Indians. They have their own God looking like them. We have Japanese. They have a God looking like Japanese. We have Chinese. They have a God looking like Chinese. Think that over. We have the Jew who does not believe too much in worshipping Idols. He still holds to Moses' teaching. He is nearer to us than any other race in the way of worship. We have the Christians who have idol worshipping. They carve out statues of Jesus and Mary, set them up in church, and tell you to bow down to them and worship them. That's a piece of wood he carved out or that is a piece of stone he carved out. Make it to look like the statue of a woman and a baby, and they tell you as you pass by to bow or cross your heart. That's a good way to do that thing too; cross your heart, and you don't pull your heart straight up and down because you are not bowing to anything like straight truth. So you put a cross across it. That means that you are cross; at the crossways of truth and falsehood.

One fellow told me one day — he said, "Elijah," he said, "you know, you go into too much definition." I said, "Why do you tell me that?" He said, "Because people don't understand." I said "Do you understand without any definition?"

Now they have Gods molded after their own fashion and likeness. Where is yours, Brothers? You don't find in America a little "nigger" God, do you? The so - called American Negro bows to everything that looks white. Now he has on the walls of his home and in his church white pictures and statues that are made by the imagination of white people. He calls them after these names: this is the disciple; this is Peter; this is Paul, or this is Mary and her beloved baby, Jesus. You are absolutely blind, deaf, and dumb. This is Mary. Yes. And he bows down and he kisses the little baby and it looks white. But you show him a Black one and he gets back. Then he wants to question you. "Oh that's not Mary's baby!" You are brought up believing and worshipping white and hating Black. "I want to integrate. I want to be the brother of you white people." That's what Martin Luther King said. When he started talking about being the real brother, then the white man killed him because the white man knows that his race cannot produce Black children!

The Black God. The Black man's God. He could not say out there to the public, between 20 and 30 million people here, he could not say: "I would like that all of us unite who are Black. He could not say that! He was a lover of white people — the people that nature did not make him to be. Nature made him to be one member of the Black People. And then after all the hell that white people have given to his people for 400 years, he comes out talking about: "I don't want to be your brother-in-law; I want to be your real brother." A man who is supposed to be a theologian, who has studied theology and the scriptures of the Bible is fool enough to tell the world that he wants to be his slavemaster's brother. I say, Brothers, you worship all the leaders you want. I am not trying to force you to follow me. I am happy without you if you are happy without me!

I only want to tell you the truth of Self. If you are Black, why do you want to be white when white came after Black? If you are Black, I say and repeat, you produced white! There was no white nor light before you. You produced both of them: light and white. You are natural - born and part of that in which you were created. You are the only man who needed light to light up Your Universe. You brought forth that light. You are walking around looking for a God to bow to and worship. You Are the God!

Think over these things. The Black man, think over that, made so blind, deaf and dumb in Africa and America that he seeks now white. He doesn't like his color. Why? Because the white man doesn't like it. He doesn't like that; he (the Black man) should have that color because that color will live forever. Praises be to Allah. I think the white man is wise. You are here today to learn in what direction you should turn to seek God — look at Yourself! Look at yourself. You certainly don't know yourself. But He Who has been born to bring you out of darkness now into the marvelous light of wisdom and understanding of yourself and your kind (the Black man's kind) knows and understands.

Should we bow to a God that was just born 6,000 years ago? Six - thousand years ago? Take that from our deportation from the Moon 66 trillion years ago. Just deduct now, 6,000 years from 66 trillion, not 66 thousand, but **trillions!** We're not talking in any thousands. We are not talking into millions nor billions, but trillions! If you don't mind, I will preach. I don't know anything but preach. God has made me a preacher. I always wanted to be one. I was about to start preaching Christianity, but He caught me before I ever started. He as good as said "Little Fool, you are yet to be taught what religion you should teach. He took me with Him for three years, night and day. He said, "Here it is, Elijah, you can go now, and I can go." I said, "Thank you." He said, "You don't need Me any more." Oh, yes, I do I need You.

Every race has a God looking like itself. But here in America, poor, blind, deaf, and dumb Originals, my own Brothers, don't have a God looking like them. He doesn't have any God at all — only the white man. Now comes the time that he should be separated from the white man and go for Self. He says, "No, no, no. I want to stay with him!" What must be done to make him go for himself? He is sold to his Master. What must be done?

Angel said to Baal and to his donkey — He said: "If the donkey had not seen me, I would have slew both of you." The donkey He's mentioning there means: "If that little dumb Messenger's eyes had not come open to the knowledge that I am God, I would have killed all of you." Because it's time, it's time that you should be killed. "But it happened that he opened his eyes and he saw Me; he recognized Me." Praises be to Allah. "I am going to give him a key. I am going to give him Keys for all of them, that he can open their cave-doors." "Open them up, Elijah, here are the keys! And tell them to come forth, that I Am here. Tell them I will set them in Heaven at once—money, good homes, friendships in all walks of life." The Black man's God. "Tell them that I have come for them. Tell them that I will walk up in a mountain 40 miles to teach just one of them. Tell them, Elijah, I love them!" "They have been here 400 years, and there is none that has befriended them. I Am their God," He said, "and I love them. I will destroy the Nations of the Earth, to save them and then die Myself." And I said, "I'll do the same." I said, "I can't destroy the Nations, but I will die trying to teach them." He (Allah) looked at me and smiled. He said, "Yes," He said, "You will do that." He looked at me some more. He said, "Yes, He will give his life." He said, "Jesus

36

didn't do anything; no more than any Believer." Well, that's right. If I say I believe in God and His true Religion, certainly I will give my life for it.

For more than 40 long years, I have been calling on you to accept Heaven at once. You are rejecting it. You want it from the white man. I say, my friends, that today you have to do something for yourself. I say the white man has done a great thing for you to give you education how to go for yourself. I again give the white man credit for even trying to feed you when you are hungry. You are begging him and won't work for Self! This is right. I say he is very nice to you because if I had a whole Nation of people into the millions and they would not go out and do something for themselves, I would sit down on them. I would.

But He nurses you like the slave or like his fathers did when you were under them in servitude slavery. He still nurses you — gives you bread and water, clothes, shelter, money, jobs, just to keep you with him. That is all now. He pulls the string if too much is coming down and turns it off. He keeps you in that position. He doesn't try to help us go for Self. He doesn't want us going for ourselves. He wants us a subject people to himself. Regardless to you being free, he stills wants you to remain with him. He will give you today, not yesterday, but today, better jobs — if you will go along with him and stay with him. He knows that this is the Days of Your deliverance. He knows that a God has visited you. He knows that God has raised up a Messenger as a guide to you. They are very wise — a long way from being dumb. It is you that is dumb. They don't want you going out building for Self. They want you to ask them to build. That means you are their slave. He doesn't want you going out farming even as much as making your own food. That means that you soon will be stuffing your stomachs with bread and meat that you raised; and he cannot profit from that. Think it over.

You want to go along with your good white folks. I want you to show me where they are good! I beg them on the last page of our paper, **Muhammad Speaks,** to let us go and give us a place just across the border here in another state somewhere. Let us live to ourselves since we cannot get along together in Peace. He won't do it. No, no, no! You may learn to do something for yourself! But, I say, it would be wise if they (the white race) would do so. But if they don't want to do so, God is here to give us a Place.

The scriptures must be fulfilled. We are between 20 and 30 million Black people here in America and have been here for over 400 years. Now the white man who kept us blind, deaf, and dumb to the knowledge of ourselves still doesn't want to see us go free. This is an open proof. I put that on the last page of our paper knowing that the white man was not going to do it. As God said to Moses: He said, "You go tell Pharaoh to let them go." But he (Pharaoh) wouldn't let them go by a long ways. (God said,) "I have to kill Pharaoh to get them." This is what happened: He had to drown Pharaoh and his army in a sea of water. They call it the Red Sea. But it's not a 'red' sea; it's a 'blue' sea. And I mean it's really blue. I looked in it and I said, "Why have reference to; not that Sea, but a sea of fire that is coming up to get Pharaoh the second he refuses to let his slaves go free. The Bible says: They refused to let their prisoners go free and hold on to them; hold them as a prey. You know what this meant there, 'hold you as a prey! So whenever the God or Your People come after you, he will say: "If you take me, you will take him too." This is what it means. I say, Brothers, the time is here, that you should think for Self. You should build up an economy for Yourself. You say, "Why should I go out there and work and grow a crop when you are prophesying Judgment?" I say, "Brother, if Judgment comes tomorrow, you've got to eat today!"

We have to do many things. This Earth was made for you. Your Father and my Father created the Earth for us — for Black people. It was not created for White people: it was created for Black people. I want you to know that; the God of the Black man.

How came the Black God, Mr. Muhammad? He is Self-created. How could Self create Self? Take your magnifying glass and start looking at these little atoms out here in front of you. You see that they are egg-shaped and they are oblong. You crack them open and you will find everything in them that you find out here. Then were there some of them (atoms out here? Well who created them? I want you to accept the Black God. You say, "There is no beginning or ending." I admit that. But we do know that they had to have some kind of beginning. But how it happened, we don't know. That's why we say that His Beginning we don't know anything about.

Imagine, you close your eyes now: imagine the whole entire visibility of the Universe is gone from you. This is the way He was born; in total darkness. There was no light anywhere. Out of the total orbit of the Universe of darkness there sparkled an atom of life. Once upon a time; but don't ask me when it was. How could that atom of life make a record of its own creation? It could not write its own creation, the record of it, because He was the First; there was no recorders around Him. He was First to record His

Ownself. How long was that? We can't tell; we weren't there. He was the only One in the whole entire dark Universe. He had to wait until the atom of life produced brains to think what He needed. How long was that? I don't know, Brothers. But He was a Black man, a Black man! Coming out of total darkness at that time, we all could say that we are produced by a white God. But there was no light nor even any white anywhere: there was All Darkness. So God revealed to me. In that darkness, which had no end to it there — that Darkness Created an atom of Life, and the Color had to be Black as there was no light; therefore, it had to be the Color of the thing that Created it! All Praise is due to Allah!

Hating Black, the late 'minute - man' came yesterday and turned you into a fool. You have been here so long that the record could not be kept on planets. They couldn't write it on the planets and make it stay there. Only you planned to betray the time that life had been in the Universe. That's all. You hate Black and are out here trying to kill me because I teach you your Natural Self. "I don't like Black." White people made you hate Black. Not so much they hated Black; they wish today that they were Black. Oh, yes, they do. I receive lots of letters from White people wanting to join and follow me; lots of them. They are wise.

How could they (white people) teach you to love Black when their Black God (Yakub), Who made them, made them by nature to deceive you? How could they have ruled if they had taught you who was the Natural ruler? They can't teach you today that you are the people, the First and the Last. They can't say that in that sense because they know you will say: "Well, then, I think it's about time to make you the last." Don't think white people are fools. They are wise. It's you who are the fool. Don't take them for nothing like ignorant people. They are wise people. They are gods of their own world. This is true. They were made to be gods of their own world. This is the truth. They have proved that they are gods of their own world. Everything that they want, they can bring it before their people and tell them "Here it is." Whatever idea that they create in their minds that is necessary for their own life to live here on this planet, they bring it into perfection. But you don't have that creative mind; that's a creative mind they have. It was taken from you 6,000 years ago to allow them to build a world after their own thoughts. I say, my friends, you won't believe it if I keep talking to you about your own God.

Now let us take a look at the white God and the Black God. The Black God produced Himself; He's Self - created. Then that Black God made the white man. He didn't create him. He made him from Himself. If He had made him or given him power to create himself, He could never rule him. He is doing a hard job at it now. The Bible teaches you in Genesis that God said: "Let Us make man." I want you to wake up. Well if somebody is talking about making a man, why did He use 'Us'? The Holy Qur'an says: "We made man." We! There's no difference in "Us" and "We." Who is that "Us"? Who is this "We?" You say, God made the man. Well, God did make the man. But why did He have that "Us" and "We" around him? Because that's impossible now. God can't make a man without a help. No, no! He was Self - created Himself, but He can't make a man without help now because the law of Nature, Creation, won't allow Him to do so. So it takes an "Us" now. It takes two people to make a man. Therefore the Bible and Holy Qur'an plainly teach you, "Us" and "We" made him: did not create him, but made him.

You don't say that you created this metal here because the essence of it is out there in the earth. You didn't create that. But you take it and melt this, the metal, out of something like stone or sand. You can scoop it up down there and sift it — but it was all ready out there. Then you make whatever you want to from that metal. But, now, go and create something! As the Holy Qur'an says; The white race cannot create anything. They use what has all ready been created. They don't argue with you about what they cannot do; but they know that they were given power as gods to rule you for the past 6,000 years and they have done that. They have built for you the necessities of life. They made clothes for you and me. They built houses for you and me: They got our bread from the Earth and gave it to us because they were the gods; not because they were so kind and good to us, but they must rule as a god. They must give the people the necessities of life because they are the gods. We had no other god to look forward to. Our God was put to sleep to let the white god rule. How could the white man rule if the Black man is going to rule while he rules? The Black man is self - created. Two Gods cannot serve at one time. Think that over.

Let's now consider this a little deeper. In the first place, one God was the God of the Universe. In the last place, One God is the God of the Universe. Everything that is of life and everything that is of metal or everything that is matter in the Universe came from Him. He created it! The Holy Qur'an says to the white race: show Us what you have created? What part of the Universe have you created? None,

none, no part! Well, then, if you didn't create all of this that you are living off, why not serve Allah then? He said, "I can't serve Him. You made Him; You made Him Black, and You made me of clay. And I just can't bow to that. I wasn't made like that. You didn't make me to serve Black. You made me to serve my white self and made Black serve me until the day that they are raised up into the knowledge of me. That will be the end of me then."

Who, I say? Never has this kind of teaching been poured into your ears since the Earth was or the Nation was. I teach you not of prophets, but of God? No, no, no. I am not preaching of Isaiah and Moses and others. Those are prophets. I am bringing to you the knowledge of God Himself!

The Black man's God. Why do you reject the Black God when the Black God is Your God! The Black God made the white god! Why do you reject Him? Long before ever there was — as the old people use to tell me when I was a little boy — a when and a where, He was God. I bear them witness today. Just think it over: a little small atom of life rolling around in darkness. Think it over: Building itself up, just turning in darkness, making its own self. Let's go into it. Do I have any proof of this? Yes sir! He made Himself into total darkness. He put His Ownself turning, turning on His Own Timetable in the Black womb of the Universe. He started rotating. He demands every life that comes into the Universe today to start turning first. "Over to Me, for I had that to do myself." "Now, I am going to see, that every life that comes into this Universe comes out of total darkness — every life!" Yes sir! It must come out of total darkness. Out of the womb of our mother did we come. We were created there out of the sperm that

43

come. We were created there out of the sperm that was emitted into that total dark room, the womb. It took that to make that child. He couldn't be made in the light. He must be made in total darkness.

We must know ourselves, we must know the Nature of Life. We must know the law of Life before ever we can say that we are Masters.

Now if, by nature, we are born in total darkness, think it over. And if, by nature, life brings us out of darkness; and if, by nature, we walk in light from out of total darkness; and if, by nature, we can think through darkness, and bring light out of that darkness by our own brains, we did so with the white race. Look right into the sperm of life and find him—here's an unalike. Take it! separate it! Your first separation from white and Black was done. Now, you say, "No separation will settle it." It won't settle it with you, maybe, Mr. Fool, but it will as once upon a time you ·could not see out of Darkness. Now, today, you can't see out of Light.

Who was it that did this? Was it a white god or a Black God? It was a Black God! That is Who did it. He had taken His Universe, (think it over), and engulfed it with the path of light that you call the Milky Way. Think that over. He engulfed His own Universe with nothing but a path of Light. He made the lights so close to each other that the light of this one never stops before this one ties his light in with that one. It was a whole path of nothing but light, a belt around His Universe. He thought so much of His Earth, He loved His Earth so well, that He took His own Earth and divided the live planets rotating around it with light — stars, Think it over. About 600-million miles out from this Planet, He has a region of stars that divides the other planets from these inner planets. He but stars. Think it over. He made a crown for Himself out of the Earth with stars. "This is My House, and I want to put a crown around it with stars." You tell me you don't like the Black God!

He speaks, Brothers; His Desires come to pass. He takes His Enemy, folds him up with the power of nature, and makes him beg to be let go. He speaks to His treasures of snow in the North. He tells them to "Roll down on My Enemy." — Here they come! He lifts up the clouds from the Earth that He made and the water that He made on it and bears them up to a certain height and tells them to pour it back down. Can you do that? This is the Black man doing that. He drowns out His Enemy; floods His enemy out; takes His Sun: "I made you, Ball of Fire, 853,000 miles in diameter. Sun, go out there and burn up the crops; they don't like Me. Burn up that grass out there that their cattle are eating." And the cattle begin to grit their teeth towards the Sun, begging for more rain. The Sun says, "I have orders from my Master; settle it with us."

What hopes have you in the future of the White race? I want you to tell me that. Write it to me: 4847 S. Woodlawn, Chicago, Illinois. Write it to me. What hopes do you see? Today right at this hour, they are destroying themselves. They are fighting trying to bring about Peace, and there is no peace for them. They are talking Peace, but the Old Prophet says: "Whjle they talk Peace, the sword reaches to the sword." It's going on. Do you see any future for them? They don't have any, here nor there. The time of that clock has run down, and the hand is stuck on six.

I am not trying to make mock, nor am I trying to be happy in that way because of their destruction. Their destruction means your destruction in the condition

45

you are in. You are a disbeliever, and that means you will be destroyed. The thunder of war is now engulfing civilized Earth like a belt on a man's body. Nowhere is there a sign of Peace but in the Nation of Islam.

He created the Heavens and the Earth. How did He do it? First, He created Himself and He was Like of Himself. He emitted light from the live atom of Self. And they still can do that. They can crown you with light. I say, my friends, wake up. The Black man does this. He creates as light out of darkness where there was no light and calls forth light to come. "I Am here, and all around Me is darkness. I need a Light." The Sun, having come into existence, started to shine. He didn't have to go get wood, coal or gas. He just said, "Come on Sun." She refused to stay back, and She brought Him warmth — heating that dark Universe, and then giving Him Light. Later, another One says, "I think I need another Light over here. There, Be a Light." They kept on saying, "There, be a light." until They filled the space with so much Light that you can't find a telescope that will take you to the wall of darkness. You can't see out of Light." I must not disobey my Master one second." The cattle say, "We're dying for grass." Allah says, "Yes, but if the rains come, and you fill your belly full of grass, you will fatten. And the Devil will eat you. Then the Devil will rob the poor man of price for you that he didn't feed; I fed you! He won't give Me credit for growing his corn, his hay, and producing your food that you may be fat in his stalls. But he will take you and set you on the market for a high price. And My poor People are begging for your flesh. But I have got to stop your flesh in order to stop him. Burn them up! They don't believe in Me. They didn't create the Heavens and the Earth. They didn't create the clouds.

46

They didn't create you, little animal. I created you; I caused you to grow! I put water in the Earth for you. I put food in the Earth for you. But you are fattening off what I give to you; and he is commercializing on My Own Property and causing My People to suffer."

We went over the country trying to buy beef - cattle to sell to ourselves. He (the white man) says, "No, I am not going to cut one penny for you even if you buy a hundred - million tons — the same price." He goes down in the South, he does, sits, looks over our people's little herd and crosses his legs, "Bring them on here. Oh yes. I will give you so much for that." Don't even tell them to weigh them. "Oh, yes, I'll give you $200.00 for them." Think that over. But when he gets them in the North, he says: "You will not smack your jaws on this beef until you pay me my price." Getting it for probably 10¢ a pound on its feet, he is selling it for 45¢ and 47¢ wholesale. Then you have to sell it for 55¢ to $1.65 per pound to try to get anything out of it. I say, let us unite! Build up our own economy! The white man makes it impossible for you and me to live in Peace Together. He robs us until we have to lay down on his doorstep and beg him for existence. I say the day has arrived that we are going to get up from your doorstep. Regardless to what the cost, we must get up! We have to raise us some cows. We have to raise us some sheep.

Let them go to work and multiply. When they multiply, let us take them and eat them ourselves and feed our people on them. The time is here that we must do for Self. Stop laying at the white man's gate, begging him. He says you are free. Show him that you can take this freedom. Make good of it for Yourself by uniting and doing something for self. Go to Your Black God. Stop looking for a white god to take care of the Black people. They just don't do it. It is not in their nature to do these things. They are not going to make you independent. No, I should say not. If you get independent, you will have to do that yourself!

You are no national; you are no citizen of this country! The only citizen here is white. You are not American; the only American is white. You can't be American unless you are white. But you can be a slave for the Americans. Brother, I don't mean to make you feel bad. Mr. Politician, who thinks you are smart and know the law, I don't want you to think that I am trying to make fun of you. But you are yet ignorant to the fact that you are not a citizen. You are not a National man. National means "to be citizens of that country," but not a slave of that country; and especially not to a foreign slave — he comes from abroad! Think that over. "Well, I was born here." Yes, there are many people born here: English, Swedes, Germans, lots of them born here, but they have a country that they are citizens of. But you don't have a country that you are a citizen of. You have to make yourself now a citizen of Africa, your native country. You can't go back there calling yourself "Mr. Willie Jones." You can't go to Africa today and get good friendship with them. They are afraid of you. They say that you are just another white man under a Black man's skin. They don't want you. But if you say you are a Muslim, they want you — they spread out their arms for you if you say you are Muslim. We know. We have been there. Our Secretary here, and my son standing here, and myself, we have been there. They are visiting me almost weekly. I have asked them right before my own family and others there at the table with us, "Would you take them if they were Christians?" They say, "No." They don't want any Christians. This is what has ruined their country — Christians!

You say that Christianity is your religion and it was the religion of God and Jesus. You are just as silly as you can be! If you read your Revelation, you will find out how Christianity came about. Read it in the Bible, that last little Book. If you don't understand it, come to me. If I tell you for understanding, and if I miss it, I will give you $10,000 out of my Brother's vest pocket — paper lined.

You nurse the Bible. You nurse the enemy of the truth of the Bible. You worship him while the Bible teaches you against worshipping the Devil. Well, (you say) "He is all right with me." How is he all right with you when he's not all right with your people? You can't make yourself one of them unless you graft yourself back into them. You'll still bear the seed. I want you to remember this, my Friends. I am not making fun. I only want you to to know Your God — Your Black God. That's all I want you to do. Just know Your God. And I want you to know the white god.

Now, you say, Christianity is your religion. You don't want anything else. Offer you anything else and you would rather be an atheist now than to accept anything else. This is the truth. "Oh, I don't believe in any of it." An atheist, (he thought he was an atheist), came and had dinner with me one day. And I laughed inside. I said, "Now, you poor fool, how can you prove that you are an atheist?" And so, I looked at the man and started talking with him. And when he went out, he admitted that he was a fool for ever believing like that. You can't be an atheist except if you are a fool. But if you wake up and get wise, you can't be an atheist.

My beloved Brothers and Sisters who are thinking yourselves Christian, you are not Christians! You

49

can't be a Christian unless you are white. That is the only race on Earth that is Christian; white people. I say, today Christianity is in an awfully terrible condition. The Father, the god, sitting in Rome, is in a terrible condition trying to keep his people together. Look at how they are now, demanding him to give them something new. Don't you see their Bible being fulfilled? And look at the name that the Bible gives to that man — a Dragon. The Pope of Rome is spoken of in the Bible as a Dragon. Think it over. And the people that he serves, as Beasts! Don't go out of here angry with me because I say what you wrote yourself. This is what the white theologians and scientists of the Book or their religion wrote themselves. I got hold of a little book once on the argument between the Pope and Martin Luther over some of his symbolic work that he was doing in the Bible. And they began to question what this meant and what that meant. You would be surprised. I don't have time to go through everything in detail. But God has given me the knowledge of the Book. And therefore, I wish to tell you that you are so wrong in calling yourself Christians. You are so wrong! There are no Christians but the white man. I'll tell you the true meaning of Christian which refers to us, the Muslims. "Christian" means to be crystallized into one. Christians are not crystallized into one. They say, "We are followers of Christ; that is why we call ourselves Christians." Where are your works if you are following Christ? And who is Christ? They say, "Jesus Christ." What Jesus Christ? Jesus wasn't even a Christ back then, 2,000 years ago. According to the meanings of 'Christ' that name means One coming in the Last Day or Crusher — He Crushes the wicked: Christ, the Crusher. Jesus didn't do that. That is the Mahdi who will do that today; the One whom we are representing to you; The Great Mahdi; the Restorer of the Kingdom of Peace on the Earth.

You should remember that the time of wisdom, now, is coming for you. And creative thoughts, now, are coming to you. And the God Who has chosen you to be His People will teach you and lead you how to fashion them into actual beings as the white man has done. Our creative thoughts were taken from us until he (the white man) rules his world under his own creative thoughts.

But he had to use the same material that Our Father put here. He (the white man) wasn't able to create his materials because everything was already in the Earth. Therefore, when he was made, he had to use what we, Our Fathers, had made to fashion him a kingdom of the material that was all ready created. And now, when it comes to us worshipping the Gods, I say: A Jesus, A Christ, A God, that Is Born for you and me today! Who is He? He is what they call, 'The Son of Man.' Who is the Son of Man? And why do they call Him that? Because He Himself is coming to Judge the Original Man and the mankind. The mankind is the white race. The Original Man is not a mankind. Don't get yourself mixed up in that kind of representing — all mankind. You are not a 'kind' of a man; You are the Man! This is what I have been teaching you here. You will try to take me to task, but you can't because you don't know what material to use. As I say, I am teaching you of the God, not of the prophets. I am the Last of them.

We want, and we must have, some of Our Good Father's Earth — a place for ourselves to live on; we must have it. We cannot live under or in this other shadow; We cannot do that! It is time that we live ourselves, under and in the shadow of our Own. All of this big old Earth here. Think over how big it is. It's a great big old Earth. They are trying to practice birth-control over you. What do you look like accepting birth-control? When has the Earth got too small for you? There is actually plenty of Earth for us. There has never been an exhaustion of the Earth or of the food that it burns out; it goes back down and fertilizes the Earth without aid. But everbody wants to live in Chicago; naturally someone will get hungry here. There is not enough food in Chicago to feed everybody. But that is no reason to start killing babies; just to live in Chicago. That is wrong; the Holy Qur'an teaches us. Birth - control is not even thought of in Islam. If this is our Earth, and it is, we haven't over - populated it. We still have plenty. You say, "China." Well, China is a little grafted race of people, and they are piled up there in that country. They can't spread out so much because they have a boundary to the race — the Red, Yellow, and the White races, There is a boundary set for them. And this boundary, now, has been jumped by them. This is causing trouble. This is why the Original Owner decided He would take over His Part. When He takes over His Part, there will be no part left for any other part!

Your Black God. Why shouldn't you love Him? Look at how He made you to verify the Truth that He is God. There was never One before Him. He made the axis, the Heavens, the Earth, and the spheres that float around the Sun to bear Him witness — "I am the First."

Look at the ball of your eye. Think it over. That ball of your eye is white, all around a black. A Black sphere there, sitting, surrounded with white. Not the white in the center of this ball; it's Black here in the center. But white around the Black. Right? He has made it like His Universe — around Him is light, but He Himself is Black! All praises are due to Allah. Look into His Eyes. His eye tells you who He is. And all the offspring from Him bear witness that I came from that Black center there in His eyes. They bear witness that their eye testifies to the truth that it must have been grafted from yours because it is not the equal of your eye. All praises are due to Allah! Would you trade your beautiful Black eye, surrounded with the beautiful white, for a green-blue eye? Would you do that? No, you won't. It is a more beautiful eye, Black. Clear Black, and clear white around it like His Universe He made. He was Black inside, and then He said, "Let there be Light—"**On The Outside.**" It is an unending teaching to teach you about your Black God.

He has power that He doesn't have to go and fix up mechanically to produce. But he says, "Be" and there it is — coming into space. **Be!** There it is. Just orbits, just burst out of space. And in a few billion or trillion years, there they are. He takes and puts Him a planet far out on the edge of the power of the Sunlight, and warms it. They call it Pluto or Plouton. Pluto is a scientific name representing 'A Little Fool.' It comes back to you and me. For 400 years we are off from our people, frozen - up in the power of the white man. We could not rotate according to the light and power of the wisdom of our Own God. Pluto sits out there, something like four - billion six - hundred - million miles from the Sun; but still just a touch of the Sun moves her. Think that over. The Sun has so much power in her that she just touches Pluto on Her equator and makes her to make the same speed of rotation as all the other planets. All praises are due to

Allah! A sign of you and me. The white race just knew she was out there in the same year that Allah found you and me. A coincidence, you call it. No, no, Something else was behind that. Why are they just learning about the Moon? For 6,000 years, they have not known anything about that dead piece of our Earth floating around this one — until today. Why didn't God let him up there years ago? Because the Black God is going to make a change now. This is true. Whenever He gets ready to destroy people, a powerful people who have ruled people; the Holy Qur'an says: "He takes him up and lets him peep into some of His Wisdom." (Allah says,) "Look at this planet here, little Enemy, I made it. Can you make one like it? (The Enemy says,) "No, Sir." "Go back to the Earth then, and pretty soon I'll be down there and seep you off then."

They (the white man) wish that they could make the Moon a resting place to shoot their arrows at God and His people if they attack the Earth. They talk about a way - station. Russia and America are after each other under their skin. Russia is pretty smart; America is as smart. We like them both smart like that. Russia goes and saddles the space right around the earth to watch America! That is who she is watching. America wants to watch God because she knows that Daniel said that she would be the One that God would get first. She knows the Revelator, John, said that she would be the first that God would destroy. The Fat Beast that everybody is frightened of, kill him first, because He has killed my people! I must tell you the Truth! The time is here! It is written, but you didn't understand it. I saw the Beast take him. (Think over these prophecies) and the false prophets with it. I saw that Fourth and dreadful Beast that rose up on the sea and land. I saw him take him.

Both prophets bear witness. He was taken, and his body was given to the burning flames. That is the prophecy of Daniel. And I saw behind this Beast the Ages of days sinning. Think that over. The color of his head was white as snow; kinky like lambs' wool. The color of his hair shows how ageable he is. Think it over. He is an old, gray-headed man — been here a long time! Think it over. His hair is not wooly, it is not animal-like; it is curly hair, it balls up and twists up. Who is he? Daniel says, "He is the Ancient of Days?" "He is the First. I can't count His Days. I don't know the number of the years, but as He was of Ages' Time. He is the coming in after this one. Praise are due to Allah!

You don't like your God? You don't like Him? You don't want a Black God. That is Who Daniel said is going to rule. Praises be to Allah. Let us love Black. I love Black. A color that you can take and put anywhere - even the North pole and it will be the same! Put it on the Equator, put it in the jungles of Africa, in the hottest zone of our planet — it is the same. But all other colors fail when changing them into various zones, but not Black. Why should Our God, Our Father, create Himself of a color that would change by the climatic conditions of His Planet? You have the best color! You have the best eyes! You have the best teeth! Oh, no. But they're robbing you of them — mechanical tests, pulling out your teeth, and putting all types of dope around and in the gums, destroying those pearly - white teeth; the most beautiful teeth in the human head. All praise is due to Allah!

I say, "love Black." I say, get together Black, and unite, Black, as never before. They try to destroy the beauty of Black and have just about done so. And they

look at you and laugh. But, still, go out there today —
right now — and you will see every color out there
looking at the Black woman. They want her! She's the
best walking in the Sun! We're going to take her;
we're going to tie her up at home. We know she is the
best, We're going to tie her at home and set the
bedsteads on her if necessary to keep her there!
We're not going to let her run rampant — not like wild
animals. She is too good, she is too beautiful!

I say, love your God. He is a Black God and He is
forever and forever. There is no such thing as trying
to destroy the Black man. You can't do that. It is
impossible! One of Our God-Scientists, 66 trillion
years ago God taught me, tries His best to satisfy His
mind by trying to destroy us. But we are here today,
and we see His idea right up there — they call it the
Moon. That is what He tried to do. Now there is no life
on that Moon. He didn't allow anyone to be left to
write His days of Himself and His great Wisdom of
Himself. We wrote it! We will do the same by you.
You won't be able to write our doom, but we can write
yours. All is set for this thing — before you ever were
created or made. He looked into you before you were
born, saw your thoughts, listened to what you would
be saying today and saw your works. We just fold up
our own arms, and sit down, and wait for Time. Allah
said, "They just waited. They're so glad that the day
has come now that they can show you now that the
Black man is God!"

This is a day and time that you should know God.
There are two on the scene at the present time: An
evil God and a good God. When we say "Allah," that
Name means God and covers all Muslims. All
Muslims are Allahs, but we call the Supreme Allah
the Supreme Being. And He has a Name of His Own.
This Name is "Fard Muhammad."

"Fard" is a Name meaning an independent One and One Who is not on the level with the average Gods (Allahs). It is a Name independent to itself which actually means One whom we must obey, or else He destroys us. This honorable, Majestic, Person comes in the last day. The reason why we call Him the Supreme Being is because He is Supreme over all beings and or is wiser than all. The Holy Qur'an teaches: He is wiser than them, meaning all the Gods before and all who are now present.

Now, the Just and Righteous One is on the scene to take His place to rule the people in righteousness.

Remember, Allah means Gods. Many Muslims go in this Name. All Muslims go in the Divine Supreme Being of Names from Him. The meaning of these Names are Himself. The Bible teaches you and me that He would give us His Own Names, and this, we are receiving.

You have the white man's name, and the white man's name is not to live. I don't say that just here alone, but I will say it in London. I'll say it in any part of the Earth I go, and they will bear me witness. That's why they don't care what they are called. You can call white men fish. You can call them cat. You can call them lion, birds, bees, anything — he doesn't care because he knows his name is not going to live anyway — it is the end of him! He cannot go in the Name of God; these names such as I am called by live forever. It's me — not a name just called by me. Muhammad — that name will live forever. The meaning of it is: One that is praised, and praised much. It will live; that is God's Name. And your Bible says, "He will give to you and me His Name, and all that take His Name, they shall live." So all that have taken the name of the Enemy of God, they were seen going down in a lake of fire with him."

I warn you to join with me. I warn you that is (the fire) is not going to be ten, fifteen, or twenty years from now; it is going to be soon!

Have you ever seen times like they are now? A President going, running all over the world, trying to find peace for his people. He may mean well, but that doesn't mean anything to the Finger of Time that wrote it and is saying in his writing that: Mr. white man, the year 1914 was set as your end. And you will have a short — a little short stay — and that little short stay, after it's done, will be it. When America comes out of Viet Nam, don't shout — the big trouble is just beginning.

They can't help it. Don't hate them because they are devils. One of your Gods made them like that. I don't hate a white man just because he is a devil. He can't help himself. He was made like that, and I cannot remake him. The Sun is setting; I can't remake him— takes too long, 600 years. It took our Brother 600 years to make him. Six days, there in the Bible, means 600 years. Everyday there represents 100 years in making the man. Now to make or graft him back into that which he was grafted out of would take another 600 years. Why, Brother, we could build on our planet many many millions of babies. You don't have to graft anybody. We make them plenty babies. In 600 years, there would be so many babies that there would be babies' babies. We don't have to graft anybody to you. They haven't been that good for us to graft them!

Be sure to get onto your own kind; that is, if you want to live! Live in your own — the Black people and under the Black God Who believes in Mercy, Justice, Equality and Peace. I am not begging you now because it is immaterial to me. I can get a whole Nation besides you. I can! He (Allah) has offered that to me. He said, "If not One goes with you or believes you, Muhammad, come on and bring Me the Keys, and you and I will go."

Don't be too proud of yourself, Mr. Politician. Don't be too proud of yourself, Mr. Black Educator. What are you looking forward to—to keep you going? I think they're knocking the pillars out from under you. Don't be too confident and proud, Mr. Preacher. I think your Bible is going to burn up.

It is not predicted in your Bible that somebody will come outside of America to lead you! Right here, under your feet, will rise up that man who will lead you. These people have no knowledge much of themselves. I am raised up here to teach you of yourself and others and of the God Who created the Heavens and Earth and His Powers — and I am not alone. I say to you, don't forget! Try and join onto your own. Let's go and get some of this Earth that we can call our Own. Let's build a Kingdom of our Own. I say that to you.

Moreover, I pray Allah that we die not unless we are Muslims. Give your families, your babies my best love. Tell them the Messenger's praying that they grow up in the Faith of their Black God, Allah; and in His True Religion, of entire submission to His Will — Islam; and that they live, as we live, in the Faith of Allah.

CHAPTER 12

Allah, God, The Supreme Being

"Oh, my servants, there is no fear for you this day, nor shall you grieve."

The fear of displeasing the slavemasters, who are the enemies, haters and murderers of the lost-found members of the Tribe of Shabazz, is causing millions of the American Black people to suffer, and they finally will suffer "hellfire" for this fear!

The aim of Islam, which is now being preached throughout America to the fearful so-called Negroes, is to remove their fear of the slave-masters which is the greatest hindrance to their salvation.

"This day", as referred to in the above verse (meaning in the time of the presence of Almighty Allah among the lost-found members of His people, lost for four hundred years from their native land and people), is the end of the time of the white race.

This race of people was not created to live on our planet forever; only for six thousand years.

They are the only people on our planet whose time is limited. We can clearly see today why Allah limited their time. It is because of their mischief-making and their causing bloodshed. It is impossible to live among them in peace. They are the world's meddlers and snoopers. They are not contented to live alone without "snooping" around and meddling in other people's affairs. Even though you divide the earth equally with them, they want your part or try to run your own business for you the way that they think best.

The so-called Negroes will never get rid of the fear

of their slavemasters as long as they believe in the white race's religion and follow the scared preachers and politicians. You should not fear today.

You will not fear if you will only believe in Allah. His religion is Islam. Follow me! Islam is the religion our salvation. You will soon come to know. There is no future for you and your families here!

Of all the knowledge that one may have or obtain, the knowledge of God is the greatest and the most necessary of all knowledge. I would say that 98% of the people of earth are without knowledge of the God, the Supreme Being.

The Christians and most old world Muslims are alike; not having a true knowledge of the Supreme One, referred to as Allah, and God makes most people believe that God is something other than a man.

Looking at God's creation (the universe) and His creatures without number and unlimited, we have never been able to obtain the knowledge of just how God created this Universe and Himself.

We have never known where He Himself began or who was first, God or the universe? Just who is God? What is He? Is He of the essence of this universe or some invisible power, spirit, or force that has no equal comparison in His creation?

The knowledge of God has been kept a secret by twelve men on our planet for many thousands of years. The twelve pass their knowledge on from son to son, but the number possessing this knowledge is never more than twelve; and they are not to ever reveal it.

The wisest of scientists have worked, studied, and searched all their life long for the actual knowledge of God and have failed to obtain it. Finally, they formed their own opinions of God.

Many claim that there is no such one (God) and that the Creation of the Universe came by chance. Man's creation, they say, took place from some lower form of animal life of the sea. But they were never able to prove such theories. Therefore, the people formed their own ideas of God, for they had no true knowledge of God.

How could we know God if He kept Himself from our having a true knowledge of Him? Just what was the purpose of this secret knowledge of God?

We just could not know God unless God made Himself known to us, and there was a set time for Him to make Himself known. Why was there a set time? It was done to keep from interfering with the rule of the devils who also had a set time. The devil is the God of the wicked (the Caucasian race) whose world must be destroyed to allow the World of Righteousness to best set up with the God of Righteousness as its ruler. For He has not ruled universally for over six thousand years. Therefore, we have been without the true knowledge of God.

The Bible's prophets make a prophecy of His coming and not of His presence and only of the spirit of God, not as a person. Therefore, the people worship the spirit (joy and gladness) of God as being the real person of God. They do not believe in the reality of God; only in spirits, wood, stone, iron, gold, silver, Sun, Moon, and Stars. Some even worship beasts, animals, and fowl, snakes, fire, and water as God. This nonsense is to be broken up in these days by the presence of the real God in person.

I am with Allah to convince the world that He is God in the person of Master Fard Muhammad and that idols are things, not persons. According to the Bible and Holy Qur'an, God is referred to by the pronoun

"He," never as "She" — always in the masculine term.

All these scriptures show that He sees, hears, feels, tastes, smells, talks our language, walks, stands, sits, eats, and drinks. Therefore, God must be a human being. He must be a human being, a man since we all refer to Him as being our Father.

Everyone looks forward to seeing the coming of God but who has prepared to meet Him on His coming? What do we expect to see, a spirit? Well we just cannot see spirits. We can only feel the spirit. Will we see a man? The world does not believe that God is a man. What are we to see for God if He is not a man? Let us check on the Bible and Holy Qur'an and see whether or not we should see a spirit or see a man for God.

"In the beginning God created the heaven and the earth." (Genesis 1:1) "All praise is due to Allah, the Lord of the Worlds" (Holy Qur'an 1:1).

The above is said by representatives of God and not directly from the mouth of God although the words are true. The whole of the book called Genesis of the Bible is said to be Moses' Book and what Moses said of the history of God's creation; and of Adam, Seth, Enos, Methuselah, Lamech, Noah, Abraham, Lot and Melchizedek.

Now God has not addressed Himself to us in Genesis, the opening book of the Bible; it is His Prophet, Moses. The Holy Qur'an's opening chapter is a prayer said by the Prophet Muhammad and all Muslims.

Here God is represented as being the One due all praise; for He is the "Lord of all the worlds" while Moses says that He is the "Creator of heaven and earth." But the prophet did not say who was God's creator. Nor does the Holy Qur'an tell us.

The Bible reads that He is the "first and the last;" so does the Holy Qur'an. The Holy Qur'an, in referring to God, uses the pronoun "we" far more than the pronoun "I". The "I" is used in the opening of the second chapter: "I am Allah, the Best Knower." (2:1)

He addresses Himself to us as being the "Best Knower"; but what we want to know is: who is this "I am"? And who is this "we"? Is it a man, or the spirit of man, or a spirit without man, or any living creature of the heavens and earth?

The Bible says "Enoch walked with God (Genesis 5:24). "God talked with Noah" (6:13) and to most of the prophets. Can He be a man or other than a man? God said that "His spirit shall not always strive with man for that he also is flesh" (Genesis 6:3).

We have a great subject before us to open up to the world. So have patience and, by the help of Allah, I shall prove to you that God is man.

The Nations of the Earth expect the coming of a God Who will overcome and destroy all idol gods and set Himself up as the Supreme God over all; for all nations have made their own gods according to the Bible (Kings 17:19).

Many people have been saying for a long time that God is already with us. Most of the people believe God to be a "spirit". If He is only a spirit, it is not necessary for us to ever see Him; only to feel Him, for a spirit cannot be seen. And this has been the only God that we have had in the past.

Let us search the Bible and see if it teaches us to believe in the coming of God to be a spirit and not a man. The Bible teaches us of the spirit of God in many places; but only once do I find where it mentions God as being only a spirit (John 4:24). And this came from a Prophet (Jesus) and not from the mouth of God.

If one reads the previous verse (John 4:23), he or she will see that even Jesus could not have believed God to be only a spirit in these words: "But the hour cometh and now is when the true worshippers shall worship the Father in spirit and in truth; for the Father seeketh such to worship Him."

Here it is made clear that the "hour cometh." This "hour" cannot be referring to anything other than the doom or end of the devil's wicked world of false worshippers who claim that they are true worshippers of the true God but are not. For the Father (God) seeketh true worshippers. So Jesus could have only been referring to the time of the presence of God, in Person.

The world of Satan, the devil, did not convert people to God according to the parable of the wicked husbands whom the Lord let His vineyard out to (Matthew 21:33; 41). In the 42nd verse of the same chapter, Jesus makes another parable of the true worshippers under the "stone that the builders rejected"; that it became the "headstone."

It is the so-called Negroes who have been rejected by the builders of governments (civilizations) who are now destined to become the head in the new world (or government) under the Divine Supreme Being in person.

It is natural to say that God is the Spirit of Truth, of Life. It is natural to say such and such a one is a liar, but where there is no one to tell a lie, there is no liar.

So it is with truth or the spirit of truth. If there is nothing to produce the spirit, there is no spirit; nor can we know the truth without someone to teach the truth. Where there is man, there is the spirit. Where there is no man, there is no spirit, for the spirit cannot produce itself.

We cannot expect to see that which cannot be seen. A spirit cannot be seen, only felt. It is like electricity. Electricity is a power produced by friction from a substance that has such power (electric) in it produced by the sun and moon upon the earth. It is not seen, but we know what makes it. So it is with God.

We know that God exists and is All Wise, All Powerful, and that this quickening power called spirit is from Him. But who is this God? A spirit cannot think, but thinking can produce spirit. So according to God's own words, through His prophets, He must be a man. He is interested in man's affairs according to the Bible (Genesis 1:27): "God made man in His own image and likeness, both male and female."

If we believe that alone, that God created man in His own image and likeness, that is sufficient for us to expect God to be nothing other than man.

A father has pleasure in his son and in his son's affairs because his son is a part of himself and his very image and likeness. There is no true scripture that teaches us that God is something other than a man. The Bible teaches us (Hosea 11:9): "For I am God and not man; the Holy One in the midst of thee."

Here the latter part of the verse makes it clear that God is a Holy One (man) and the man that he is not is an unholy one (man). This only means that the Holy God is not the wicked man's God (the Caucasian race).

Ever since Adam, the Caucasian race has been referred to as the man-made man or race and mankind; the world has taken this to include all men.

"No man hath seen God." (I John 5:19). This is another confused teaching to the ignorant masses; for if no man hath seen God, then there is no God for you and me to look forward to seeing on the Judgment Day.

If such is true, how will we know Him since no one has ever seen Him? But we do know Him and what He looks like. "We know that we are of God, and the whole world lieth in wickedness " (I John 5:19).

The whole world of the white race is full of wickedness and this is the "world" referred to. We are not of this "world" (the white race or devils) nor is our God the God of this world of devil." Our God is One today, as we had only one God in the beginning. "In that day (this is the day) shall there be One Lord and His name One " (Zechariah 14:9). This refers to the time when the true God is made manifest. Before His manifestation, the people worship what they think or what they want to be their god. The devil's teaching is a division of gods — three gods into one god. The Hindus have many gods.

The Muslims worship one God — Allah. "Say: He, Allah, is One God." Yet 99% of the old world Muslims think that Allah is only a "Spirit" and is not a man. Then they too need to be taught today the reality of Allah.

Certainly He is one God, but not a spirit," for a spirit cannot be said to be "one God." If god were only a spirit, we could not say that the spirit will come only after the rule of the devils, the wicked; for we have had the spirit all the while. A king that has no equal in power or no associate, that king will rule the world until a superior one is born.

CHAPTER 13

God in Person; Not a Spirit!

According to the dictionary of the Bible, Teman, a son of Eliphaz, son of Esau by Adah, (Gen. 36:11, 15, and in the I Chronicles 1:36). Now if Habakkuk saw God come or coming from the sons of Esau (Eliphaz), then God must be a man and not a spook.

If Habakkuk's prophecy refers to some country, town, or city; if there be any truth at all in this prophecy, then we can say that this prophet saw God as a material being belonging to the human family of earth, and not a spirit.

In the same chapter and verse, Habakkuk saw the Holy One from Mount Paran. This is also earthly, somewhere in Arabia. Here the Bible makes a difference between God and another person who is called the Holy One. Which one should we take for our God? For one is called God while another one is called Holy One. For this Holy One, glory covered the heavens and the earth, and the earth was full of His praise.

It has been a long time since the earth was full of praise for a Holy One. Even to this hour, the people do not care for holy people and will persecute and kill the Holy One if God does not intervene. In the fourth verse of the above chapter, it says: "He had horns coming out of his hand; and there was the hiding of his power."

Such science used to represent God's power could confuse the ignorant masses of the world. Two Gods are here represented at the same time. (It is good that

God makes Himself manifest to the ignorant world today).

"The burning coals went forth at his feet" has a meaning; but what is the meaning? The ignorant do not know. "The burning coals" could refer to the anger and war among the people where his foot tread within the borders of the wicked. (Here God has feet—spirits do not have feet and hands). This Holy One does not refer to anyone of the past—not Moses, Jesus, nor Muhammad of the past 1300 years.

"For this Holy One measured the earth, drove asunder the nations, scattered the mountains, the perpetual hills did bow, cushan in affliction, the curtains of the land of Midian did tremble." (What is meant by the curtains trembling?) (Who is cushan?)

"The mountains saw thee, they trembled." (Who does this mean?) "The sun and moon stood still in their habitation." (What does this mean?) The answers to the above questions are easy when we understand who this God called the Holy One coming from Mount Paran is.

The 13th verse should clear the way for such understanding; for it tells us why all these great things took place on the coming of the Holy One from Mount Paran. It says: "Thou wentest forth for the salvation of thy people (not for all people); for the salvation with thine anointed (His apostle).

He wounded the head out of the house of the wicked by discovering the foundation unto the neck (by exposing the truth and the ruling powers of the wicked race of devils). "Cush" or "Cushan" represents the Black nation which is afflicted by the white race.

"The curtains of the land of Midian" could mean the falsehood spread over the people by the white race and their leaders trembling from being exposed by the truth; "the mountains" represent the great, rich, and powerful political men of the wicked; and they also are trembling and being divided and scattered over the earth. "The Holy One" is God in person, and not a spirit!

The Holy One coming from Mount Paran (Habakkuk 3:3) is not a spirit, but God in person. Jesus referred to Him as being the Son of Man (Matt. 24:27)—not the Son of Mary, Whom He was and whom the Christians teach us to look forward to seeing on the last day.

If there is or was any truth in looking forward to seeing the return of Jesus (Mary's Son) whom the Bible claims was killed two thousand years ago, what contradicts this prophecy of the coming of the Son of Man?

The prophecy of the coming of the Son of Man by Jesus compares with other prophets, and especially Habakkuk 3:3. "Jesus saw the coming of the Son of Man as a light coming from the East that shineth unto the West." "Habakkuk also saw the Holy One as being a light as well as being Holy" (Habakkuk 3:4).

Some of the Arab scholars say that the Holy One mentioned by Habakkuk (3:3) coming from Mount Paran refers to Muhammad— and they are right. But it does not refer to the Muhammad of the past but to the One Muhammad prophesied of in the Sunnah who came from His family in His name under the title, "Mahdi" (meaning the Guide, the Restorer of the Kingdom of Righteousness).

This Holy One called "Mahdi" or Muhammad coming at the end of the world would come from the East out of the present Holy City, Mecca, Arabia, which is the East.

This is the only holy place we know of that can

produce a Holy One. Neither of the past two prophets, Jesus nor Muhammad, taught the people that they were Holy Ones, nor did they say that they were from heaven. Jesus himself denied that He was good; the only one good is God (St. Luke 18:19).

The Holy Qur'an and the history of Muhammad teach us that Muhammad was only a common Arab as his fellow Arabs were until he was missioned to be an Apostle of Allah; as was the case of Moses and Jesus who were before Muhammad.

All three of the prophets (Moses, Jesus, Muhammad) prophesied of the coming of a greater one than they. The belief in God being a spirit and not a man goes back to many thousands of years according to the word of God (Master Fard Muhammad) to me; and especially to the days of Yakub when he was grafting the white race.

This man, Yakub, taught his people every trick that he thought would help them in ruling the Black nation up to the time of the coming of God from our nation. Without the knowledge of the history of our people before the making of the white race, you will never be able to really understand who God is. With the teachings of the prophets and their histories, it is really foolishness to believe that God is other than a man.

Let us quote another prophecy of Jesus on the coming of the Son of Man: "But first must He suffer many things, and be rejected of this generation" (Luke 17:25). The words, "this generation," is not to be taken to mean the generation in the days of Jesus and His rejectors, the Jews, two thousand years ago. It means the people and generation of the Son of Man who would reject Him in His day of coming to reclaim His lost-found people; and at the same time, suffer

71

persecution of Self and His teachings as Jesus was by the same enemies in His time.

For He further says: "As it was in the days of Noah, and in the days of Lot they did eat, they drank, they married wives, they bought, they sold, they planted, they built; even thus shall it be in the day when the Son of Man is revealed" (Luke 17:27-30). It is being made manifest that He is God and yet a man and not a spirit; for these things are now fulfilled as you and I see them that have eyes to see.

I think I have made it clear to you that if we look forward to seeing or meeting God, He must be in the form of a man. The Christians' Bible bears me witness that God is a man of flesh and blood. The Bible predicts God coming as a man (Luke 21:27; Matthew 24:30; Revelation 1:7, 14:15). There is much proof in the Bible to support my claim that God is man. That is, if you want proof.

You have been taught so long that God is not a man, so you have become hardened against believing in anything other than what you have been taught. "Every eye shall see Him" (Rev. 1:7).

No eye can see spirits. The above chapter says: "All kindreds of the earth shall wail (shall be sorry to see His coming) because of Him." Never was this so true as it is today.

The wicked world of the white race today actually does not want a God of Righteousness to set up a government of justice and righteousness, for they love what they have—wickedness, sport, and play. Therefore, they are sorry and angry (Rev. 12:12, 13).

The devils see His hand at work and they are so upset that they are even preparing their own destruction while thinking that they are preparing for the destruction of others. The devils have been and still are leading the people away from the true God and His true religion, Islam.

They never wanted Islam for their religion because they cannot live the life of the righteous. And they do not want the so-called Negroes to believe in it nor pray to Allah. Why? Because Allah will answer prayer, and believing in Him and His religion will not only get us universal friendship, but will get divine aid and help against our enemies.

We need a God who will help us and answer our prayers when we call on Him; not an unknown mystery God, not a dead crucified Jesus of two thousand years ago. But we must remember that to get something worthwhile, we must be willing to sacrifice all that we have.

The prophecy of Jesus (Luke 21:12) of the sacrifice and trails to be made by the so-called Negroes could not be expressed in a clearer language: "But before all these, they (the devils) shall lay their hands on you and persecute you delivering you (the Muslims) up to the synagogues (churches) and into prisons, being brought before kings and rulers for My name's sake."

It refers to none other than the so-called Negroes who accept their own religion, Islam, and a divine name from Allah. We are the hated ones in your midst and are persecuted for no other reason except that we are Muslims—under other charges such as our not joining on your side after truth and righteousness have come to us, and knowing God face to face as we know each other's faces.

Shall we go back to that which He has brought us out of? No! As it is written: "Shall the throne of iniquity have fellowship with thee, which frameth mischief by a law? They gather themselves together against the soul of the righteous and condemn the innocent blood (the so-called American Negroes) Psalms 94:20, 21). And again it teaches, "Can there be fellowship with light and darkness?"

Let the American so-called Negroes return to their Allah and His religion or suffer what was poured upon Pharaoh and his people for their opposition to Moses, the servant of Allah.

CHAPTER 14

The Light of Allah

1. Say: I seek in the Lord of the dawn; 2. From the evil of that which He (Yakub) has created; 3. And from the evil of intense darkness when it comes; 4. And from the evil of those who cast (evil suggestions) in form of resolutions; 5. And from the evil of the envier when he envies (Holy Qur'an 113).

The dawn of a new day has arrived to seek our place in that which is new. We must have a guide. Allah (God) has always provided guides for those who seek to walk in His path.

We should hasten ourselves to the light of truth as we hasten to get ourselves into the light of the day (the sun). The light of Allah (God) is even greater than the light of our day (the sun). We must learn to be intelligent enough to distinguish truth from falsehood and seek refuge in the God of truth.

If we shall know the truth (John 8:32) and that truth will make us free, we can truthfully say that we already have long since known the truth that Jesus was referring to was yet to come and not in his days (John 16:8, 13). If that truth had been revealed 2,000 years ago, there would not be any falsehood in the world. However, Jesus, being a prophet, foresaw the devil's rule. "Seek the end of the devil's rule. Seek refuge from the evil of that which He (Yakub) has created."

The Father (Yakub) of the world created a world of evil, discord, and hate. If you do not agree with their evil - doings, your goodness is then called hate or infidelity and you are called peace - breaker.

This world of Christianity has gone mad and they think that every cry is against them. They are like robbers who have robbed and are afraid that they will be recognized by their victims. Thieves know that light makes them manifest.

Since Christianity has falsely claimed Jesus as her founder, she is now being plagued with spiritual darkness and confusion. Under such darkness the Prophet and His followers (the Muslims) are warned to seek refuge in the light of Allah (God); for under such spiritual darkness the wicked seek to persecute and kill the Prophet of Islam and His followers.

They are mad and cannot see, nor hear the truth. So they call the truth false and the false they call truth. The truth (Islam) has angered them (Christianity). "And the nations (Christianity) were angry. Thy wrath is come. The time of the dead, the mentally dead Black nation — expecially the so - called Negro, must come into the knowledge of the truth of their enemies and the enemies' false religion that was used to deceive them. They shall give reward unto Thy servants, the prophets, and the saints, and will destroy them which destroy the earth" (Bible, Rev. 11:18).

The white Christians and Jews are the guilty race. They have persecuted and killed the prophets of Islam and their followers (the Muslims or Black people in general). Now should not they be destroyed or get what they put out?

CHAPTER 15

The Days of Allah

We are living in the Days of Allah (God). This means that Allah (God) Is Present and He Is Laying a foundation for a New Government—a Government of Peace and Security for the righteous—a Government that will not be left to the scholars and scientists of this wicked world lest the scholars and scientists of this world try and build the same thing that they have already built; for they do not have the knowledge to build anything different.

The world (of the white race) is doing what it was made to do—to try the righteous with wickedness and filth. The white race cannot do any better than what they are already doing. So we do not argue and quarrel with the, which they, by nature, are made to do. I repeatedly teach you this — that you cannot change the nature of the white man unless you graft him back into that which he was grafted out of. This is what Jesus means in the Bible Ju. 3:7 in his conversation with Nicodemus. He told him that in order to enter the kingdom of heaven he must be born again because in Jn. 8:44 (Bible), Jesus had condemned all of the white race to be devils, and their father was the devil. There was no good nor truth in the father that made the white race. So when a thing is what it is by the nature in which it was made or created in, you do not change it unless you go altogether back to the material that it (he) was made out of. So this demands a rebirth. Jesus was right — a rebirth—born again, all over. Some of the clergy and the scholars of Christianity take this to be a spiritual rebirth. But it means that the actual flesh and blood that was discussed in this conversation between Jesus and Nicodemus has to be changed. Then when the man has been put back into what he was taken from, the spirit of that which he was put back into will come to him as the spirit to do evil comes to him now in what he is made in. For he was made out of evil. The white man was not made to obey Allah (God) and to seek after His Righteousness. So, therefore, to make the white man one of the righteous, the white man has to take on a new birth — the flesh and the blood has to be changed.

The reader must not take it for granted that all people are made of the God of Righteousness. When you have never learned the two Gods you think the God of Righteousness made both evil and good people.

Since the white race had the privilege to translate the Bible, they fixed the Bible's translation not to read in such way as to condemn them as being what they are. That would make people not follow them. They could not trick the people.

But let us leave the white race alone for a while and turn to our own Black self. The white race has done what their father made them to do which was to rule us for six thousand (6,000) years and rule us under that which was other than Righteousness and Justice because their father did not make them of the essence of Righteousness and Justice.

These are the days of the change of worlds since the time of the God of evil and his people is up. The God of Righteousness is now Taking His Place to Reign and He Will Not Accept those of us who are unrighteous.

Take a look at the change of names. The Bible teaches us that He Will Accept those who are called by His Name. And some of us are so foolish as to say, "What is in a name?" Everything is in a name. The Bible teaches us that all of these Names of Allah (God) are more valuable than fine gold, because in the Judgment they will save your life from being destroyed.

All people who do not have a Name of the God of Righteousness and Justice will be destroyed. Read your Bible; it is there in the last Book. Revelations warns you that all who have the name of the beast are pushed into hell-fire—all of the beast's disciples or false prophets such as the preachers of the Christian religion and those who are helping the beast to deceive us, as they are deceived. Read your Bible. It teaches us that they were blind teachers who could not ldad a seeing one, nor could they lead another blind one; for they are blind themselves.

The Jesus in Matthew (Bible) condemns the clergy - class and even prophesies that they will not receive the understanding of the truth until the very last. It even honors the)harlot as being over the preachers and as being more righteous than the preachers of the Christian religion. For the harlots understand and accept the truth when it came to them while the preachers try to condemn the truth and fight against it. Reverend, I would not be in your shoes today even if they were made of gold and diamonds. Christian preachers, the mark and the name (of the beast) referred to in the Bible are only the mark and the name of the caucasian (white) people.

Brother preacher, do we see where they are trying to be good? Do not we see what kind of evil world they have set up and which they are trying to maintain teaching your (Black) people to do all kinds of evil, murder, lying, rape, and stealing because they (white people) are like that? Why do not you teach your people against following him and do not follow him yourself?

We do not allow a Black Woman to come into our Temple wearing a mini-dress. Why do you let them come into what you call your 'holy temple' of God (church) indecently dressed? You are not respecting the God, you are disrespecting Him, when you allow His followers to do all kinds of evil and to go filthily dressed. You do this because you like it yourself.

The Holy Qur'an teaches us that the devil leads you only to evil and filth. This is referring to the white race and you see this going on now. Their world is a world of sport and play. All day and all night they try to keep you busy on some sport and some other foolishness such as games of chance.

Preachers, you are making a poor job of trying to reform your people. Why do not they come to me? When they come to me, you see a difference in their actions, in their talk and the way that they dress because it is the Spirit and the Power of Allah (God) in the truth that I teach them, and they change themselves.

If I were you, I would lay that poison book down which you do not understand, and come and join up with me and we will soon have a new nation here. But as long as you oppose me, you will be spiritually blind until Gabriel blows his trumpet. Remember what the Bible teaches you concerning your seeing and understanding the truth in the Last Day—that the preachers and the priests will be the last to understand because they are the ones who try to condemn the truth and keep others from believing. So Allah (God) Is Just in blinding them so that they cannot see and understand.

The Days of Allah (God). These are the Days of The Son of Man and the days of the removal of the old world of evil, filth, and unrighteousness. These are the Days of setting up a clean world under the guidance of the Original People (Black Nation) who were never guilty of doing evil until one of the gods by the name of Yakub discovered the essence of the Black Man to make a white man and Yakub did just that—he made the white man.

Now since he has discovered this essence, today we are under the God (Allah) to do away with that very essence in us so that no other man can make another people who are different from us. This will never happen again. That is why you are taught that you will be born again physically. This rebirth is in order to get rid of that wicked material in the very essence of the sperm of the Black Man. This wicked material will not be in the Black Man for any one to use after the removal of the present world and people.

You will be caused to grow into a new person and the nature will be different. It will be the nature of righteousness and then we cannot sin. In that kind of rebirth it will be impossible for us to sin.

So the days of Allah (God) mean the setting up of a new world and a new people. Allah (God) Will Not even accept the names that we used in the old world.

The Holy Qur'an teaches the scholars like this that I am about to write—I say the scholars for the average reader cannot understand it —that after the removal of this world—after twenty (20) years you will not be able to follow and do that which you are now following and doing in this world today. Within twenty (20) years the thought of this world will vanish from your mind. You will not even be able to remember what this world looked like or what went on in it. Your mind will be clean. Ask the wise scholars and scientists. They will agree with me.

Do not look for a spirit, a spook, or a formless thing. The formless is what we think in our brain. It is formless until we make a form for it. We cannot use a God or follow a God that is not something like ourselves; for if He Is Not something like ourselves He Cannot Have an Interest in our affairs.

Therefore the Bible prophesies and the Holy Qur'an also teaches us that a Son of a Man will Come to us to be the Judge of the Judgment Day. This Son of Man Will Sit As Judge. Why He Is Called the Son of Man will have to be taught to you. Here I do not have the time and the space to teach you why He Is called the Son of Man.

The days of Allah (God) mean 'years' of Allah (God) and not a twenty-four (24) hour day. It means years. These 'Days' or 'years' of judgment, according to the Bible and the Holy Qur'an, will not run over twenty (20) years. And according to the scientists of Islam the teachings of the Holy Qur'an, which are to be understood, the Judgment is to take place between 1380 and 1400 years after the death of Muhammad the son of Abdullah.

And according to the scholars and scientists of Christianity, they have it just about right too. The time that they say the Judgment will come is based on two thousand (2,000) years after the death of Jesus. This is right. And in the Bible, in the Books of Daniel and Revelation, the time is given, if understood.

So we use a very quick and simple word that covers all that I have said concerning the Judgment and the Judgment Day or time of the Judgment that we are living in. And these are the days of Allah (God), the God Who Will make a new heaven and a new earth after the removal of this world, god, and people (wicked).

I am mighty sure that from what I have said here you will see the very necessity of the God changing our way of thinking and then He will change our name and give us a Name, for we never had a name of our own. All of the names that we have been going in are the names of our slavemaster (white race).

Now, Black brother, Allah (God) Demands you to go in your own Nation's Name. Those who are in the Names of Allah (God)—these Names are telling you their very nature and the Power of God. There are about one hundred (100) Different Names of Allah which take up all of the Attributes of Allah's (God's) Power and the Nature of God.

The only white people who have a name that is any good are ones who have of these Names of Allah (God). A lot of white people go in the Names of Allah, for there are a lot of white believers in Islam. I have met many of them and they are sincere in their faith. There will be quite a few thousand in America. When the time comes you will learn of them, but you will not learn of them at the present time.

Just remember how evil has made you. It has made you foolish and ignorant to the knowledge of good. And you make mockery of good and you worship evil. This is why the Bible calls you blind, deaf, and dumb. Spiritually you cannot see and distinguish truth from falsehood and you are not interested enough in the truth to listen to it. And you are not capable of speaking the language of truth and you do not practice righteous intelligence.

All of this was done to you and me by the white race who were not created and made righteous. Therefore they taught us that which is of themselves, evil.

We try to teach some of our people Islam who have never heard Islam before. The first thing they want to do is to start making mock of it. That makes you look pretty ignorant to dispute that of which you have no knowledge. This is what we meet with in our people. They dispute without knowledge.

Even white people do not dispute with us, for they know Islam. Islam is the Arabic name for the righteous people whom you call Muslim. Accordingly the word in the English language means 'submission'—and we add—'to the Will of Allah' (God).

The days (years) of Allah—we should be happy to see Him take to Himself to Reign in Justice and Righteousness today since we are the children of the God of Righteousness.

For this is what we lack—we are not even free to do Righteousness. As long as we do not know righteousness, there is no such thing as Justice for us. You are justified in this world of the white race for being nothing but a fool.

As the Isaiah put it "none called for justice and none sought justice and justice was trampled under foot." He was so right in his prophecy.

Let us unite upon the base of Righteousness. And when we agree to live under the Law of Righteousness we will learn to love each other. We cannot treat each other right unless we love each other. We cannot love each other until we know self.

The God Has Raised me from you and in the midst of you to give you the knowledge of self. You will not find me making a mistake in teaching you the knowledge of self. I am so sure of the truth of you and others that I always offer a reward of $10,000.00 if you can find one word wrong that I teach you in the knowledge of yourself.

I am not to make a mistake in teaching you, for a mistake in such teaching will put the people into a fisher's net and you will be cast into hell-fire.

The days of Allah. These are beautiful days. He Created you to be the righteous. He Came to you to Bless you and to Give you the Reward of the Righteous. That is why He Forgives you for your sins that you committed with the white people. He Blots them out and He does not remind you of them if you will turn to righteousness. He does not even mention the acts of evil that we did under the white man, for He Charges the white race as making us an evil, and unrighteous, and a filthy people.

Let us glorify Allah (God) and Make Him feel happy for visiting us with Freedom, Justice, and Equality and the ncessities of life. Do not you think that we should be happy of a God who Gives us what we have been wishing for and striving for all of our lives and which we were never able to get?

I say, let us accept Allah (God) and follow His Messenger so that we successfully live in heaven while we live.

MAY THE PEACE OF ALLAH (God) BE WITH YOU WHO BELIEVE.

CHAPTER 16

Day of Resurrection of Dead
So -Called Negroes Has Arrived

I don't have to say to the so-called Negroes that hell is for them in the white man's Christianity!They know it and have experienced it in this Christians' hell. The white Christians and their religion which they falsely say and teach is from Jesus is, in reality, from the Pope of Rome who is the head of the church, and not Jesus. Therefore my people can never hope to be successful with their white enemies acting as their religious heads and guides.

The false Christian religion is for the white race and not for the Black nation. Islam is our religion. Allah is our God and the Author of Islam. No Black nation can be successful trying to play the white race's game of civilization. They will only be trapped as slaves.

Islam is a religion of divine power and will give power to the helpless so-called Negroes to overcome the devils and their false religion, Christianity. It has never helped the so-called Negroes against the white Christian's brutality. Black Africa should have learned her lesson from it and driven it back to Europe and America where it belongs. The white Christians preach that Jesus, whom they killed 2,000 years ago, will hear and save the so-called Negroes. Let them prove that lie! How can a dead man hear and save people? You are not taught to pray to be heard by Moses and other prophets, not even Elijah whom they say went to Heaven whole soul and body. If Elijah cannot hear a prayer and he was not killed as Jesus was, then how can Jesus hear a prayer? We must not pray to dead prophets. They can't hear our prayers.

The Muslim loves all of Allah's prophets, but we will not pray for life to come to us from a dead prophet; not even to Muhammad who lived nearly 1,400 years ago. We pray in the name of Allah and mention the name of His last prophet in our prayer as an honor and thanks to Allah for His last guide to us.

The day of resurrection of the dead so-called Negroes has arrived. They have lived overtime in bondage to the white Christians. The white Christians will not accept Islam, for Islam is a religion of truth, freedom, justice, and equality. They have lost the power of attraction and rule over the Black of Asia and in their frenzied effort to restore it, they are now running all over the world trying to deceive the Black nation so as to allow them time to continue their wicked rule of injustice.

We must do our utmost to keep our nation pure by keeping the white race away from our women. We're proud of our Black skin and our kinky wool; for this kinky wooly hair is that of the future ruler. Look into your poison book, Dan. 7:9, Rev. 1:14. It has been boasted that America is a white man's country, but why did they bring us here? If the white race is such a super race, why don't they live alone and leave us to live alone in our own country? Why are they fighting to stay in Asia? Why not be satisfied with Europe and America? We didn't ask to be brought here.

Mr. White Christian, tell us who brought you and your race into civilization when you were walking on all-fours, climbing trees, living in the hills and cavesides of Europe just 4,000 years ago? Was it one of your super whites or one of our Blacks? Who put you there? Was it yourself or did we put you there?

Where did your race first see the Black man—in the jungles of Africa or across the border east of Europe in beautiful cities and homes? Who did you find in the Western Hemisphere, your people or our people? Who created the Heavens and the earth, my fathers or yours? Who created your race, yourself, or one of my nations? Can you claim this earth or any other planet to be that which your fathers created!

Who started the dust storms in your country? Who is quaking your country, your kind or Allah? Drive us out and see how long you will remain. But if we drive you out, we will live forever without you as we did before you. Let the white race keep silent about who shall live on this planet, for they haven't anything. This is our earth! Be happy, white folks, that you have the so - called Negroes in your midst, and especially those who are Muslims, for if they were not, you wouldn't last very long. But they shall be taken from you. It is binding upon Allah to fulfill His promise to Abraham that He would return them again to their people.

CHAPTER 17

A Few White People Are Muslims By Faith

It was Islam, through Moses, that brought the white race out of the hills and cavesides of Europe. It was Islam (as revealed to Muhammad of nearly 1,400 years ago) that again gave you spiritual crutches with which to walk after your weakness there in what is now known as Turkey and the Balkan States in Europe.

There are white people in Europe who believe in Islam. They are Muslim by faith and not by nature. They believe in righteousness and have tried, and are still trying, to practice the life of a righteous Muslim. Because of their faith in Islam, Allah (God) Blesses them and they will see the Hereafter.

There are quite a few white people in America who are Muslim by faith. Good done by any person is rewarded and these white people who believe in Islam will receive the Blessing of entering into the Hereafter.

The white people who believe in Islam will not enter the Hereafter that is Promised to the Lost-Found Black People. The Lost-Found People will take on a new birth.

But the white people who believe in Islam will not take on a new birth because they will not be the people to live forever. Because of their belief in Islam, they will escape the great world destruction that we now face.

The white race (devils) have deceived the darker people of the earth by implying that they came from

89

the God of Righteousness and that they are equal with the righteous, by having been created by the God of Righteousness.

The white race is not equal with darker people because the white race was not created by the God of Righteousness. The white race is not a created people; they are a made people. They were made by Yakub, an original Black Man — who is from the Creator.

Yakub, the father of the devil, made the white race, a race of devils — enemies of the darker people of the earth. The white race is not made by nature to accept righteousness. They know righteousness, but they cannot be righteous. Jesus made this clear when he was trying to reform the white race (devils) two thousand (2,000) years ago (Bible, Jn. 8:44).

If you and I believe that the devils are from the God of Righteousness, we are making the God of Righteousness an evil god, who created an evil god, and made the evil god to become the best guide for the people of righteousness. The God of Righteousness Would Not Make an enemy of righteousness as the best guide for keeping the righteous people on the right path.

Allah (God) Master Fard Muhammad, to Whom Praises are due forever, Comes in Person, to teach us the right way and to point out to us the great arch deceiver (white race, devils). That the white race is a race of devils is the most hated truth that they are opposing in the last days (resurrection of the mentally dead).

This is the Judgment of this world of the white race. They are bringing themselves into the Judgment of God, Himself, by trying to take vengeance, in the Last Days, on the Apostle of Truth and on his followers.

Remember these words, (Bible, Is. 65:15) ... "The Lord God shall slay thee (the enemies) and call you (who submit to His Will) by another Name." Glory not in the name of satan, but Glory in the Name of the Lord God of Truth Whose Name abideth forever, and His Names have the Most Beautiful Meaning.

Now Allah, The God Of Islam, Invites us to accept Islam.

Holy Qur'an

"And who is more unjust than he who forges a lie against Allah, and he is invited to Islam.

They desire to put out the light of Allah with their mouths, but Allah will perfect His light, though they may be adverse.

He it is who sends His Messenger with the guidance and the true religion, that He may make it overcome the religions, all of them, though the disbelievers may be adverse."

CHAPTER 18

Be Yourself

Allah's great teaching and warning to us (the so-called Negroes) is: "Be Yourself." What is our ownself? He answers that "Your ownself is a righteous Muslim, born of the Tribe of Shabazz."

He taught us that we are the original people of the earth who have no birth record. He calls on us to submit to him that he would set us in heaven at once. He has made it clear what constitutes heaven on earth; freedom, justice, equality, money, good homes, and friendship in all walks of life. This Christianity cannot give us (not the Christianity that has been taught to us).

He greatly rejoiced over us and was very happy that He had found us. He said that He would make a new people out of us who submit to Him by causing us to grow into a new growth; not an entirely new body but a reversal of the old decayed body into a new growth which, He said, would make us all as we were at the age of 16.

There will be no decay in this new growth of life. He also stated that the next life is a life of unlimited progress.

He taught us the things that were and are and a glimpse of the things to come. His fiery warnings of the judgment of this world make one feel as though there will be a very, very narrow chance for any life to survive such a destruction. He taught us that our foreparents were deceived and brought into America by a slave trader whose name was John Hawkins in the year of 1555.

Just what happened to our foreparents and us, their children, after landing here in the Western Hemisphere would make a dog weep and fight that her pups were treated in such manner as our forefathers and their children were treated.

Our first parents who were brought here, he said, were killed after giving birth to their first babies to prevent them from teaching their children anything of self or of their God and people.

This act of murdering our forefathers (by the slavemasters) left their children to be taught and reared in whatever pleased the slavemasters and we are from those children. That made us blind, deaf, and dumb to the knowledge of self or anyone else and it stands true today that the American so-called Negroes don't know themselves or anyone else and the worst of all is that they don't know that they don't know themselves or others.

We can't be considered a free people as long as we are in the white slavemasters' names; this the white man never advised the so-called Negroes to do, but yet he claims that we are free. He also refused to teach us the truth of our kind, their civilization before bringing us into slavery.

The knowledge of Allah, the Supreme Being, the true religion (Islam) had never been taught us by anyone before the coming of Allah in the person of Master Fard Muhammad.

The whole of the Western white civilization is opposed to Islam, the only true religion of God; therefore they (devils) don't teach of Allah and Islam to us. He said Christianity was organized by the white race and they placed the name of Jesus on it as being the founder and author to deceive the Black people in to accepting it.

After our first parents landed here they saw that they had been deceived by the devil, John Hawkins. He brought them here on a ship named "Jesus."

This ship was on its way back for another load of our people. Our forefathers started at the old slave ship as it departed, and they begged to be carried back. But it was to no avail. And our forefathers said to the whites: "You can have this new Western world, but give the ship "Jesus" back to our people and country." This has now become a song among our people which goes something like this: "You can have all the world but give me Jesus."

But our poor foreparents did not know at that time that it would be 400 years from that day before the real ship Jesus (God Himself) would come and get them and their children and cut loose every link of the slave chain that held them in bondage to their slavemasters. This would be done by giving us a true knowledge of self, God, and the devil. And 400 years of tears, weeping, mourning, and groaning under the yoke of bondage to the merciless murderers would be wiped away.

The slavemasters' children are doing everything in their power to prevent the so-called Negroes from accepting their own God and salvation by putting on a great show of false love and friendship.

This is being done through integration as it is called; so-called Negroes and whites mixing together in schools, churches, and even through intermarriage with the so-called Negroes. And because of this, the poor slaves (the so-called Negroes) really think that they are entering a condition of heaven. But it will prove to be their doom. Today, according to God's Word, we are living in the time of a great separation between Black and white. The members of every

94

nation must go to their own, and the American so-
called Negroes are the most handicapped in the
knowledge of just what they should expect at this
time.

CHAPTER 19

The Black Man

According to the teachings to me of man's histories by Allah (God) in the Person of Master Fard Muhammad, praise is due to Him forever, The Great Mahdi and the Messiah that the world has been expecting to come for the last two thousand years, has come and is going about His work as has been predicted that He would do.

He taught me for three years (night and day) on the histories of the two people, Black and white.

What He taught me verifies the teachings of the Bible and the Holy Qur'an (if rightly understood) of the two people, Black and white.

He said that there was no birth record of the Black Man and therefore none can say how old the Black Nation is. As far back as, He said, a record has been kept, it dates 76 trillion years. These years (76 trillion) were divided into periods of six trillion years beyond 66 trillion years which would make the said figure 76 be 78, instead of 76 trillion. I will not go into the finer details here. I hope to go into the details and an analysis of our Lord's (Master Fard Muhammad's) teachings to me in a book entitled **Black and White.**

Allah, in the Person of Master Fard Muhammad, to Whom praises are due forever, taught me that there are not any gods Who live forever. Their wisdom and work may live six thousand or twenty-five thousand years, but the actual individual may have died within a hundred or two hundred years, or the longest that we have a record of, around a thousand years.

There is no God living Who was here in the Creation of the Universe, but They produce Gods from Them and Their Wisdom lives in us.

Human Beings are created according to the life of the Universe (planets). Master Fard Muhammad, to Whom praises are due forever, taught me that the Original Designer and Maker of the Universe created it on time and there is an end to it.

Scientists have learned by study that everything we see that we call Universe is not everlasting. It is gradually decaying. The Bible and the Holy Qur'an both verify this decay of the Universe and that one day a Wiser God than Them all will exist in a new Universe. A new universe means that it will not be exactly like this one that we know. According to the hints of the Holy Qur'an, it will be a better one than we have. Naturally, after experimenting with a thing that has been made, we can improve on a new make of it.

The Black Man's Gods, according to the history He taught me, have All been the Wisest. They made the white man after their order in wisdom except the knowledge of how to bring into reality and perfection their vision and idea of what they want to perceive equal to the Black Man's Wisdom. This was kept back. They are forced to build their world on the basis of what they found in the Wisdom of Black Man.

The white man only made, formed, and put into service those things that met with the cravings and necessities of his people.

The white man was given the power of vision and different ways of life to enable him to build an unalike world from what we have had throughout the millions, billions, and trillions of years.

No God Who is going to rule the people of earth universally, as the white man has ruled for the past six thousand years, was to be given a history or knowledge of the God Who ruled the people before Him. This is in order to keep the Present God from patterning after the Former God and to force Him to use His Own Wisdom in making a world and not a world patterning after previous Wisdom of the Gods Before Him.

The white race did not get a chance to rule solely according to their wisdom because we were present and they patterned much of their world after what they saw of the Gods of the Black Man. This was due to the fact that the white race was made an enemy to the Black Man; therefore their time to deceive the Black Man was limited to a short span of six thousand years that are used by the Black Gods to rule.

The Wisdom Of Each God, according to what Allah (God), in the Person of Master Fard Muhammad, to Whom praises are due forever, taught me, has a cycle of twenty-five thousand years.

Once every twenty-five thousand years, another God would be given a chance to show forth His Wisdom to the people.

This has been going on for many trillions of years, according to His teachings to me—at least since the deportation of moon and earth, according to the science of why we use a cycle of twenty-five thousand years. This is compared to the circumference of our earth at the equator, which is approximately twenty-five thousand miles. This is also compared with the rotation of our earth or the change at the poles which also makes a complete change once every twenty-five thousand years.

The White Race is an unusual people and their ideology is unusual. He has and was given the gift of a creative mind. To allow him to use his own ideas, the

Black Man or Gods were put to sleep in order that the Wisdom of the Black Man did not interfere with what the white man is made for (to rule us under wickedness, enslavement, deceit, murder, and death for six thousand years).

The Black Man or gods of the Black Man are infinitely wise. They are being aroused to their Wisdom today to rule the people again throughout the ages of time.

The Present God's (Master Fard Muhammad's) Wisdom is infinite. No Scientist can see an end to This Man's Wisdom coming in the future. That is why the Bible and the Holy Qur'an refer to Him as The Greatest and Wisest of Them All and say that He will set up a Kingdom (Civilization) that will live forever.

The Black Man in America is not an example of the Original Black Man; for he has been used by his slave masters for four centuries in what we call experimentation. Through the experimentation by the wicked slavemasters who were made without love or mercy for Black people, they have the Black Man in America before the world as a wrecked, robbed, and spoiled human being without knowledge of himself or anyone else. And he is used by the white man as a tool for whatever purpose the white man sees fit.

He is called a "Negro" by them. The name means something dead, lifeless, neutral (not that nor this).

They call the slave after their own names because he is the property of the slavemaster until he is redeemed — although he is a member of the Original Black Nation.

To restore him back to his people, he must be re-educated to give him the knowledge of self and the knowledge of those who deprived him of the knowledge of self.

This knowledge of self will unite him onto his own kind with love of self and kind.

CHAPTER 20

Why Black Man Should Be Called
By the Names of God

The Black man from the root beginning is from a Black Father. Therefore, he should go in the Name of his Black Father.

As I have said, as long as the so - called American Negro is blind to the knowledge of self, he does not know by what name he should be called. You could call him anything and he would answer to it, for he does not know his True Name.

The white man calls the so-called American Negro by many nick-names. The so-called American Negro then re-nicknames himself the nick-names of the white man, although he does not even know what they mean.

The Black man (so - called American Negro) is a member of the family and a direct descendant of the Creator Who made the Heavens and the Earth. Therefore the son should be called by the Name of his Father and not called by the name of an alien. The white race is an alien people to the Black Man.

So many times you have heard that God has ninety-nine (99) Names or Attributed (That Which Is Attributed to God). The 100th Name or Attribute of God is the Name, Allah, Which Represents that He is All in All, of every Good name. His Name Begins with the Name Creator and Ends with The First and The Last, The Eternal. Many of His Attributes refer to such Names as Power, Force, The Mighty, The Wise,

The Most Merciful, The Maker, The Fashioner, The Best Knower, The All-Hearing One, The All-Seeing One.

The Holy Qur'an says that He has the Best Names and the Most Beautiful Names. So many of these Names that we should have are pertaining to Our Father.

His Name of Praise and of "worthy of Praise" are just a few of the Great Names Which Belong to God, and He Wants to Give Them to us. The Bible teaches us that He Will Give His Names to those who believe in Him. According to the Bible, Rev. 7:3, the Judgment cannot take place until those Who Believe in Him are Given His Name (sealed in their forehead).

Will you turn down a Great Name which will Live Forever, Bible Is. 56:5, in exchange for the nick - names of your very enemies? They have no meaning as to a human being, such as Mr. Fish. We are human beings and should not be called Mr. Fish. They name you Mr. Hog. You are not a Hog. They call you Mr. Bird. We should not be called bird. We are not winged fowl. They are names which are worthless to human beings.

The only white people who are allowed to use One of the Names of Allah (God) is one who has accepted Islam. These Names are given to them because of their faith in the religion of Allah (God). However, this does not mean that by nature these Names belong to them.

It is only you, Black Brother, that by nature should be called by the Names of your God and Father, the Creator of the Heavens and the Earth.

This is what Allah has taught me. Believe it or let it alone!

CHAPTER 21

Black and White Worlds
Near a Showdown

Due to the presence of Allah In Person, (Master Fard Muhammad to Whom Praises are Due forever) and His Aims and Purposes to take over His own, it brings us hourly to a showdown of who shall rule the Nations of Earth.

The present world (white people) have had their time and have gone over their time to rule. Nevertheless they still want to rule or destroy the idea of someone else ruling as shown by their preparations made for the total destruction of the Human Family of the Earth. They boast that they can destroy the present total population of our earth 30 times over... again and again.

We know that they will not be able to destroy it one time. But they are preparing to do so should they be given the chance. This is very hard for you to listen to or accept from a man who stands at your door telling you that he is prepared to destroy you again and again and blast you out of your own house. We are now told in many skillful and deceitful ways that the white world is prepared and is putting those preparations into action against the Black Man.

The earth actually belongs to the Black Man. This is made clear in the Bible and Holy Qur'an. The prophetic sayings of the prophets for 4,000 years from Moses have constantly warned the present rulers (white) that the day of showdown was coming and that the world belongs to the Original Owners (Black

Nation).

The white race was given a limited time (6,000 years) to be the overlord (white) of our earth and ourselves. He is well aware of it (time).The white man is well aware that he does not own the earth and that he had no part in its creation. The scientists of the white race well know this, but, nevertheless, as it is written (Bible) Jer. 49:21, we see that today trouble is brewing everywhere; even between Black and Black where it should not be. But where Black wants to live with white and does not want to take his responsibility to go for self, Black has trouble with Black due to this desire. Integration is against the Desire and Will of God Who Wants and must Do that which is written He Will Come and Do: Restore the earth to its rightful owner (Black Man).

The white world, as it goes out, has not been asleep to its responsibility. They have been building up their arms and arsenal and factories for this day, in order to kill the Black Man. They are doing this in so many ways with drugs and the surgeon's knife in the hospitals. It is the greatest desire of the white man that he does not leave the Black Man in position to keep populating the earth under his own color. Our women are the target. They want to stop them from bearing children. Millions of our women fall for this destruction of their race.

The Black Nation is under the Guidance and Guardianship of our God, the Great Mahdi, He is The Restorer, The Defender of The Black Nation. He Will Restore and Defend us.

There is nothing that the white race can think of in this day and time that is not already known by the God of the Black Nation. Therefore, the showdown will be victorious on the side of the God Who Knows what we think and plan. He has power over us and over the atoms of the atmosphere. The attacker would have no power whatsoever to defend himself in a showdown against such a Wise and Powerful God, The Great Mahdi.

The Great Mahdi has and exercises power over everything of the creation carries or brings forth power. One would be silly and greatly the loser to attack such a God. But nevertheless the world must see a showdown between the two Gods. His Eyes and Ears are ever Open in both camps...the wicked and the righteous. So these two worlds draw nearer and nearer together for a showdown.

The American Black Man is to be warned and he is warned of this showdown which is coming between the two worlds. He should fly to God (Allah) of his people Who Has Power to save them.

My work, to bring you into the knowledge of Allah(God) and the God of your fathers and the knowledge of the power of that God and to ask you to accept your own, has been given to me. The Black God is well able to give you your own.

Fly to Him, I say. Fly to me and I will guide you to Him as you do not know Him. If you do not know, seek to know. I will teach you to know. To reject your share in the earth and the universe which is rightfully your own would be such a foolish act that it could never be blotted out of your future history.

Come Follow Me, I say. I will lead you to your God of Salvation. If you stay where you are, you will suffer the consequences. Just as a reminder, read the Bible Jer. 50:46 and II Pet. 3:10. It is terrible, awful, and frightful, to look up and instead of seeing a blue sky, see a sky of flames and fire. This will surely come. Allah (God) has affirmed this prophecy with me. The whole heavens will be blotted out and in its place there will be a canopy of flame. The heavens and elements that make up the atmosphere of the earth will melt with fervent heat. There will be an explosion of the total atmosphere of the earth by God Himself. Take Heed of it, for the Holy Qur'an says such a time as we are entering into now is a grievous time. It will make children's hair turn gray. If the grief and excitement will make children turn gray because of the terribleness of judgment, what do you think our hair will be doing? The Bible prophesies gray and baldness upon all heads.

My people, stop thinking of sport and play and think over your life and the safety of your life.

CHAPTER 22

The World

The World (under the rule of the white race) that we have been living in had a duration of time of 6,000 years. We have been living in **The World** for the duration of her time, and how her time is **up**, and she (The World) is conscious to the fact that God Will Rule the people in a government of Righteousness.

The Old World (of the white race) that is now going out cannot rule the people in righteousness because nature did not give them any righteousness!

Therefore, the two (the righteous and the unrighteous) disagree with each other and they cannot live in peace with each other.

Therefore, the two must be divided, and the followers of each can go along with their own leader. The righteous will follow their own leader and the wicked will follow their own leader.

This is symbolized in the Bible under the symbols of "the Sheep and the goats." If you study the nature of these two animals, you will find that there is a great difference between them.

One Animal (the sheep) is trustworthy; and the other animal (the goat) is untrustworthy. By nature the Black People are good, but the Black Man is like a sheep— if the wrong people, the evil people, teach and guide him, he will become like his evil guide.

But as soon as you take the Black Man away from the evil guide and put him under his own good guide, he will go to his own good guide and he will follow him because, by nature, the Black Man loves good.

This is why the Bible prophesies of a great separation (of the people) coming about before the end of The World of the wicked who love to take people and mix them up and make them to believe in other than right.

As you may have learned, if there is any good Black Man in America, and if his goodness is such that he refuses to teach people to follow the guide who is no good — then the no-good man becomes a hater of that good person and seeks the death of the good person.

The no-good man speaks evil of that good man just because the good man makes manifest the no-good man. Being no-good he does not want to be made manifest to **The World** because the no-good man seeks to keep **The World** under his no-good guidance.

The Doom of The World (of the white man) and the Time when his doom will come (now is the time of his doom) but those whom he has made blind, deaf, and dumb do not know who he is nor the time that he is to be taken away.

So, therefore, The World (of the white race) is filled with confusion and they do not know that to do themselves. They have confused the Black Man to the extent that the Black Man does not know now whether he should go for himself or remain seeking guidance from the devil.

But Allah (God) Will Not Let any of us be blind, today, to the truth. This is why He Came Himself; to be sure that there will not be any mistake made. Allah (God) Makes For Himself A Messenger.

Then Allah (God) Guides the Messenger Himself. He does Not Leave the Messenger to do all of the Guiding. Then Allah (God) Sends Angels to see that His Guidance is carried out like He Taught the Messenger to do.

Great World of confusion — fighting is raging all over this **World** of those who love fighting. The proper thing that we Black Folks should do, today, is to unite together behind the Divine One whom God Approves — the One whose work is seen — the one whose work is made manifest to the eye of The Whole Entire World.

This is He Who Wrote This Book!

Hurry, Black Man, And Get Out Of The Name Of The White Man Before It Is Too Late!!!

CHAPTER 23

He (Allah) Makes
All Things New

He, Master Fard Muhammad, God in Person, will create a new heaven and a new earth, a new Islam and a new government and people. The new earth referred to is a new people who will change the old into such a great future that actually the earth will look like a new earth and a new earth will be made here in what we call America.

America is the place where the new earth will actually take place — after one thousand years of the destruction or the fire that is mentioned throughout the Bible and the Holy Qur'an. (In this, the prophecy of the Bible and the Holy Qur'an agree). America — as it is called — will be void of life after the burning up of the wicked and their world or their way of civilization so that no one will pattern after them in the new civilization of the Hereafter.

This is the way of the Gods. One God is not allowed to pattern after another God when it comes to universal change. He is to use His own Wisdom. The white man brought about a universal change and so will Master Fard Muhammad, Allah, (God) in Person, bring about a new universal civilization even as Yakub, the father of the white race, brought about a new universal wicked people and a wicked rule over righteousness.

This is what is meant by the old passing away and a new coming into existence. There was a new world of the white race that came into a vacuum in our history, from the 9,000th year to the 15,000th year of our calendar history, a vacuum made in our past 16,000 years, of 6,000 years, given to the white race to rule. We are now in the 15,000th year of our calendar history of 25,000 years.

The rule of the white race terminates at the 16,000th year and that year is the beginning of the Black Nation's rule again, as we ruled before the 9,000th year of Yakub's making. This is the beginning of what is prophesied — the 7,000th year, meaning the seventh thousandth year after the rule of 6,000 years by the white race, and in our calendar history, it is the 16,000th year (this is called the 7,000th year by the Christian writers).

There is much more on this subject that I would like to teach and write, but the space is limited.

Only the principles of the present Islam will remain the same. It is the Black man of America who is referred to as the lost member or lost sheep of his people. The awakening or rising of the Black man in America must come first because he is the choice of Allah (God) in the Person of Master Fard Muhammad for building a new heaven on earth.

They are the blindest, deafest and dumbest of people who are without the knowledge of self. They are trod under the foot of civilization as "no people," as referred to in the Bible and Holy Qur'an.

As God created the present heaven and earth out of nothing, so will God, in the Person of Master Fard Muhammad, build a new heaven on earth from nothing (a people who are nothing) so that this world will have no claim on the making of the new people of the new heaven on earth.

The universal awakening of the Black man must also take place. He is also blind, deaf, and dumb, from the touch of the white civilization. They do not know themselves. They are referred to in a prophecy of the Bible as being a sleeping lion that must be awakened.

As in the problem given to us by Master Fard Muhammad, they are referred to as a lion caged, that must be let loose. In Isaiah of the Bible, we are referred' to as a people who are robbed, spoiled, imprisoned, and a prey. And those'who have us a prey will not let us go free.

The Black man must be awakened to the knowledge of self — that he is not what the white race has taught him to be. He must come out of this hopeless state. He thinks he is worthless. He should be brought into a state of worthiness and the knowledge and reality of his great place into which Allah, (God) in the Person of Master Fard Muhammad, will put him. He is to place him on top and not the bottom — because the bottom is where he is today — and make him no more the tail, but the head. He is to become the head of civilization of the new world or new heaven or earth. He is not to rule over this people, but he is to be the ruler of self, after the rule of the Caucasian, wicked world.

You will have to look to your own God, Master Fard Muhammad, and your religion, which is peace, Islam. Islam significantly means the makings of peace, but not making peace with the enemy of peace. The so - called Negro is arising to the knowledge today that I am teaching — knowledge Allah (God) revealed to me throughout the Black man's world.

Go to Asia or Africa and you will hear more about the happiness of the people over what Allah has revealed to me than among the American Black people. They all know that it is the truth that they have been waiting to learn for 6000 years.

Read Isaiah 65:17 and 66:22 and Revelation 21:1 of the Bible. Read the second Surah of the Holy Qur'an. the new generation will be raised up.

My main mission and work, put upon me by Allah (God), in the Person of Master Fard Muhammad, to Whom Praise is due forever, is to put you on the right path so you may go for self under the guidance of Almighty God Allah in the Person of Master Fard Muhammad.

He (meaning Master Fard Muhammad) will end the present conflict between the slave and his master. If they will do anything for us of good, they will be rewarded for that good act by Allah (God), Master Fard Muhammad, and they know this.

Rev: 21:5 What Will Become of the old?

We must have a new government, a new ruler and a teacher of that new government, since it is not patterned after the order of the old government (world).

As the God of Truth, Justice, and Righteousness, Allah Is Going to Be the Ruler or the Creator of the New Government. Then by no means can He Carry any of the old world into His New Kingdom of Truth, Justice, Equality, and Peace. We must have a new government and a new people to operate the new government (Bible Ez. 18:31).

A new heaven and a new earth (Bible, Isaiah 65: 17, 66:22). Here is the mention of a new heavens and a new earth. Some of the scholars take it literally and some take it spiritually. I say the meaning is both literal and spiritual.

After the destruction of the old world by fire and by other means of destruction, there is nothing of the old wicked world that can be salvaged to carry into the new world of righteousness. Note Bible, Ez. 18:31.

The prophet (Eze. 47:12, Bible) says that Allah (God) will even make new trees and shall bring forth new fruit. Jn. 13:34 prophesies that a new commandment shall be given to us which will make you able ministers of a new testament 2 Cor. 3:6. And 2 Cor. 5:17 says that "if any man be in Christ, he is a new creature." Eph. 2:15, prophesies "of twain, one new man, so making peace."

The Bible, 2 Pet. 3:13, prophesies, "We look for new heaven and a new earth" and Rev. 21:5, "He said," 'behold, I make all things new.' "

Since the Bible here has promised through the mouth of the prophets, that Allah (God) Raised Up in Israel will be brought about when the God of the Resurrection of the Dead Appears, the Dead will no more be as they once were. They will become new creatures.

The Holy Qur'an teaches us that "He caused things to grow into a new growth." Here we have something which the Holy Qur'an says "is worth praying for." Under the God of Freedom and Righteousness, we will grow into a new growth instead of growing into decay any more.

Also in the Bible Isaiah mentions the long life of the righteous in these words: "that a person one hundred (100) years old will be like a child" ...meaning that their age will never cause them to look old. They will have the freshness of youth says the prophet, Isaiah. And the Holy Qur'an, also verifies the same. Allah (God) in the Person of Master Fard Muhammad, to Whom Praises are Due forever — out of His Own Mouth — Said to me that He Causes us to Grow into a New Growth. And that we would have the look and the energy of one who is sixteen (16) years of age and our youth and energy of a sixteen year-old would last forever.

In that new life there will be not such things as a stoppage or cease to beget children. As you may read in the Bible Noah was six hundred (600) years old when the flood came (Gen. 9:28, 29). That number six hundred (600) is very significant. Noah lived nine hundred and fifty (950) years. The Bible teaches you that he begat children all of those nine hundred and fifty (950) years.

They claim that there are people today in certain parts of the earth who are way over a hundred (100) years old and they still beget children. This is referring to the Muslim people who live in the Himalayan mountains.

On the earth, wherever it is fertile and with water and rain in due time, and in good warm climactic conditions, we find trees and vegetation produced the year round

According to Allah's (God's) Teaching to me, the age of the present earth is around seventy six (76) trillion years old. Of course the earth's material does not decay fast, but it is decaying. Science proves this.

Then the Bible and the Holy Qur'an verify these prophecies that everything will pass away or that there will be a gradual decay except Allah (God) Himself. Holy Qur'an Chap. 26:3... "everything has a beginning and everything has an ending except Allah (God) Himself." Allah (God) Cannot Be Destroyed, for He Is the Maker of the Present heaven and earth and before these are destroyed He Brings In a New heavens and a new earth or He Reproduces the present one as the Holy Qur'an teaches us.

Since there was no calculation of time in the beginning of the creation of the heavens and the earth, we do not know the exact time, but we do know that it took place. We do know that the material out of which

115

it was made will not last forever. The moon is a good sign of that decay. Since the moon has no water on it, it has become a decaying mass of once-earth with water.

What we will direct our attention to now is the type of government and people who will replace the present government and people. Since this is a wicked world and its making was not based and made upon righteousness, we cannot expect it to endure any longer than the limited time of six thousand (6,000) years. For at the end of six thousand (6,000) years the old world meets with the God (Allah) Who Came in the Person of Master Fard Muhammad, to Whom Praises are due forever, Whose Wisdom, Might, and Power are Greater Than the god, Yakub, who made this world (white race).

Yakub, the father of the white race, did not make the white race from nothing. Yakub made the white race from us (Black Man). So he took living material (Black Man) to bring out a new people. And so Will Allah, the God of Righteousness. Allah (God) Will Take living material, the so - called Negro, and make a new people out of them. The so-called Negro, the Black Man, up from slavery of four hundred (400) years, here in America, is the people out of whom Allah (God) Wants to build a new heaven and a new earth or we say, a new people and a new government.

There has been decay in the government of the wicked for the past two thousand (2,000) years — since the death of Jesus. I am positive that you see the corruption in this government which is bound to end in the complete fall and destruction of this government.

We, the Black Man in America, the once-servitude slave of white people, are now rising up. This is what the Resurrection means — to rise up — to stand up and act civil and do civil things for yourself. The fall of one government and people (white) is the rise of another government and people (Black).

The Muslims and their religion, Islam, will triumph and dominate the people of earth. We need a new people and a new mind. A new mind will give to us a base for the building of something new.

In the next life, which will grow out of the old life, there will be no such thing as sickness and drugs used in the human body for the purpose of destroying disease germs because we will not do that which will cause disease or sickness. It starts on the order that the righteous shall not eat but one meal a day or every two days and eat better food. This will prolong our life and double and triple our life-expectancy. To be blessed to see the next life is worth praying for, my Black Brothers and Black Sisters.

The New Heavens and the New Earth are coming in now. The old heavens and the old earth are going out, as Peter prophesied in the Epistles of Paul (Bible). What I would like to say here is that the so-called Negro or the Black Man in America, up from slavery has, as Isaiah prophesied, "seen a great light."

It is impossible for this world to overcome the King or Ruler of the New World of Righteousness, Freedom, Justice, and Equality. Number one... the time of the white race is up. Their time has passed. The hold-up is the slow - awakening of us, the Black People in America, and the slowness of the Black People to accept Islam. We cannot follow a recent or temporary religion. We have to have the Religion of Allah (God) in order to survive forever. Islam is the Religion of Allah (God). Islam means our entire submission to the Will of Allah (God).

We need a new everything. He (Allah) makes all things new.

Are you surprised that Allah, the God of Righteousness, Will Bring in a new world after the removal of the rule of the God of evil? The term of office of the God of evil is up. Are you surprised that you will have to accept a change? Do you love the white man's type of civilization and its doing.. that way of deceiving and murdering? Do you love this evil civilization more than you would love a government of peace where the Freedom of Man is given and where equality is not withheld from those who are qualified to be their equal?

Would you like to say to the prophets who prophesied (and their prophecies are written) that they lied when they said that this world of evil had a limit of time of six thousand (6,000) years? The six (6) work-days in their work-week are to remind them of their eventual end. "Six (6) days (6,000 years) thou shalt do all of thy work and on the seventh (7th) day thou shalt rest (die). And all of thy work shall be destroyed and thy name shalt be destroyed that this race be no more remembered among the Nations of the Righteous."

Do you think all of this is false prophecy just because you love evil and hate good?

This is not the first time that a new change has come into effect among the people. Take, for instance, their six thousand (6,000) years are divided into two's (2's). Also at the beginning of our (Black Man's) Creation, it is divided into two's (2's) and ends in the number six (6).

This is the reason that in the Book of Revelations the Bible teaches us that the enemy's number is the same as the number of the Black Man. The enemy has a number of six (6), but the difference between his number six (6) and our (the Black Man's) number six (6) is that the enemy's time of rule is of short duration while we (Black Man) can look proudly to infinity of time in our history.

He makes all things new. Who Is He and what is He Going to Make New? He It Is that Comes after the time of the wicked god and his wicked rule.

The actual Foundation Base that Allah, the God of Righteousness and Truth, is Building His New Kingdom of rule upon is Freedom, Justice, and Equality and Entire Submission to His Will.

What can Allah (God) do with this world of the white race since it has not come into his line of Guidance and government of people? There is no place for the evil practices of their evil kind in Allah's (God's) World or Kingdom of Righteousness.

To make all things new means to go to the very root of everything that exists. We are taught that we ourselves will become a new people. The Holy Qur'an teaches that He would Cause the righteous to grow into a new growth. The Bible prophesies that you (the righteous) "will be changed in the twinkling of an eye." The disciples of Paul did not know exactly what you would look like in that changed form but they concluded "you will be like Him (Allah)."

He makes all things new. Allah (GOD) Who Came in the Person of Master Fard Muhammad, to Whom Praises are Due forever, taught me that every twenty-five thousand (25,000) years, each God Coming After the Other God made a new civilization. His Belief, Teaching, and Theology were Different From the Other God Who Preceded Him Who Made a beautiful change in the History of the wisdom of man.

The making of the white race was something new. The difference between the two people (Black and

119

white) is that the white race is a made people and they have a beginning and an ending. The Black Man is a created people and we have no beginning nor ending.

Before the making of the white race, we never had their type of evil people. The Black Man was never under an evil rule. Evil was never practiced among the Black People before the making of an evil world by Yakub. We never saw or experienced a civilization like the white man's civilization. We never had an unalike people among us before the white race was made. We were all alike especially in color.

In the angels' decision over the making of the white race, they said to the Maker of the white race, "What will you make but something that will cause blood-shed...a mischief-maker in the land who will cause bloodshed?" But the Maker, Yakub, did not deny that he was making such a man; but he said he "knew what the angels did not know." He did not know what the angels did not know. The angels knew that he was about to make a man who was going to destroy the peace of the Original Man and they told Yakub, the Father of the white race, what he had in mind to do in the making of a new man from us. So does Master Fard Muhammad, to Whom Praises are due forever, Know what He is About to Do in Making a new civilization.

The new man, the white man, came from us, but he is different from us. After Yakub grafted his man (white man) from us, his man became a new man to us. We are not a part of the white man.

The white man just looks like a human being, and he is a human being but he is not kin to us at all. You say, "I cannot understand how that is, Mr. Muhammad." This is true. After the white man was grafted completely out of the germ of the Black Man the White man was made into a new man, different from the Black Man whom he was grafted from. The white man became a new person altogether and his very nature is new to us. They do not have the same nature as we have. The white man is different by nature than the Black Man and the white man has made many things new.

The white race are the gods of their world. The white man put us on wheels. You say, "Oh, but we had wheels before." That is all right if we did have wheels. He himself put you on a new wheel, one different from the one you were using for transportation. The white man moved you off the camel's back and the donkey's back and he put you onto fast-powered transportation such as automobiles and he put you on wings in the sky. All of this was new compared to what we had. So we would like to show you that the white man himself has made a new world. Therefore should we be surprised when the God of Righteousness Comes in and Makes a New World and that He does not want any material of the old evil world? Are you surprised or is it due to your desire to remain with the old wicked world? The Next World is a World of Righteousness. You do not want to be righteous. You want to have Freedom, Justice and, Equality. But you still would like the wicked to continue to rule because of your desire to be wicked.

The God of Righteousness Who Will Rule in the Hereafter Will Have an unlimited Rule and not a limited rule like the rule of Yakub.

How Must the God of Righteousness Begin? What thought do you have of Him and His Beginning? He Makes All things new. The first way to bring about something new is to change the way of thinking of the people. When you have removed from the people the old mind and idea then you can insert new ideas into their minds. This is done by the old being attracted by a new way of teaching...a new school of learning to condition their minds to that thing that you are about to present to them that is altogether new and different from what they have been accustomed to.

Should you worship the old wicked world and its wicked god or representative and allow it to exist forever and not allow a better world to come in? We cannot hinder Allah (God) in His Building of a new world because we lack the power to hinder Him. There is no god or nation with equal power to exert against Him to prevent His Idea from Becoming What He Wills them to be. Whatever He Desires He is Wise enough to Bring it to Pass. Many Times this Wisdom is misunderstood and the people think that it is some example of the person. We say, Wisdom, Power, Force! There is no Power or Force of Power until we have the Wisdom to Produce it.

He makes all things new. He teaches us that He Could Use nothing of the old world and that after the removal of the old world He Is to Bring About the New World. Allah (God) Does Not Want the old god to think that He is weak in Wisdom and Knowledge and Power to Bring something altogether new without using their old wicked material.

This is like the Creation of us. In the beginning, the God Who Created Us had no material to use to begin a creation. He Had only Himself. Therefore out of darkness and the thoughtless and invisible He Brought Out the Visible Vision and Thought and Idea. He Made a Brain which had the power to cover the sphere of our thinking and to produce from that thought what image or vision that the brain cells could conceive. These things at that time were all new; there was no plan or universe except His. This is our Father, the Black Man, the Maker.

The Wisdom, Idea, and Way of Thinking of Master Fard Muhammad, to Whom Praises are due forever, is Superior to any way of believing today. There is no one to hinder His Image or Thought for that which has not yet been conceived in our brain.

He goes after the root of all things like our Black Father did in the beginning when He Built the universe out of nothing. He Is as One Sitting out in space with no material of space to Make something altogether new. He Goes after the Root in Making this New World of people.

As He said, "first He Makes a New Mind for us and a New Way of thinking." He teaches us a different education, one that we have never had before. He Gives us Education on the Wisdom, Knowledge, and Understanding of Gods...not of prophets... but of the Gods of the Prophets of the past. He builds our minds according to the way Gods Think and not the way of thinking of servants (prophets). The prophets of the past were inspired and their inspiration was true.

For the past six thousand (6,000) years there was no god present who was superior to Yakub. Our God and Scientists were not permitted to interfere with the people of Yakub and their civilization nor in the the way in which they were thinking. That is why they (white race) would kill prophets who came among them teaching the way of righteousness to the people because Yakub's people, the white race, was not to build a civilization on the basis of Righteousness. The white race was to build a civilization just the opposite of Righteousness, and this he has done. This is the reason why the God of Righteousness and Justice cannot use the white race's way of civilization. The

God of Righteousness must remove the white race's way of civilization altogether and build upon a new Foundation, as I keep repeating. The thoughts, the minds of the people must be so conditioned into the way of thinking of that new world that we must not think in terms of the new world being a part of another old world...Even your education of this wicked world will not be a part of the education of the new world.

I think that you are thinking that I am going too far now...However no education of this world of the white race will be accepted into the new world. For the new world you have a new education and government. The God of the New World is a New God. He is not the God Who Ruled from the Beginning but He Has the Same Idea of that rule as the God In the Beginning Had to create Something new.

As you notice, the effect of thoughts or your thinking at times has such deep effect on the brain that it affects the surface of your face, skin, and body. Your eyes are also affected by that tremendous thought or way of thinking that you have as it acts upon your brain.

Allah (God) makes it very easy in the next life... that new life. You will be happy all the days that you are in it. The Holy Qur'an teaches us that "He causes the righteous to grow into a new growth." The basis or pillar of that new world is when the old mind has been changed to a new mind or our thoughts are changed to a new mind or our thoughts are changed to a new thought or new way of thinking which brings about a change of the whole body.

In the new world you will not even be able to speak the English language. The speaking of the English language by us will be stopped. No language of the wicked should be spoken by the righteous, as there are some in Islam, in the Orthodox Muslim world, whom I have met myself, and they refuse to speak English; for it is an infidel language. This is the truth. English is a bastard language, for it is a language that is made up of other languages. It is a dependent language. So we see here why it is necessary for us to have a new language.

He make all things new. Go back to the very earth, as the prophecy concerning this change goes like this. The prophets say that they "saw a new heaven and a new earth." We and the earth both will be new because the Powerful God or the Supreme Being over all Has Superior Wisdom and He Will Cause everything to grow into a new world from that of the old world.

The curse of Yakub and his people veils all of the earth and the atmosphere of the earth. After the removal of the curse of Yakub there will be a new way of thinking by a new God. He is Superior to all other gods who Existed before Him. The power of heaven and earth will submit to His Power and a change is made easy and inevitable; for the heavens and the earth are controlled by the God of the Black Man, Allah, Who Came in the Person of Master Fard Muhammad, to Whom Praises are due forever.

He makes all things new in order to keep it from being said or written that He had to borrow some of the wisdom of this world..this would make Him Lacking of Wisdom and Power to Produce something other than what had already been produced.

Therefore, the Holy Qur'an teaches us that He Has the Power to Destroy the entire universe and bring in a new one and He Can Reproduce the present universe.

I would like to say to the reader that you have that

Powerful God in your midst now. As the Bible teaches you, "He Came After the workings of satan, the wicked."

He will not even Accept you and me if we are not willing to be called by His Name. You cannot keep the present name of the wicked and be present as one of the Righteous in a righteous government.

He makes all things new. In one place in the Bible it is prophesied that "you will have a new name" In another place it is prophesied that "you cannot see the Hereafter unless you have A Name of God." This is why the white race does everything that it possibly can to keep you from being called by one of the Names of Allah (God) which consist of ninety nine (99) Names. If you refuse to accept one of the Names of your God then you are the servant of the devil and you go to his doom with him.

The Psalmist teaches you and me that the names of the white race have no meaning and value of good. They are not the Names of God; therefore these names of the white race and the people who go in such names as Wood, Fish, and Bear will be removed. The people of Righteousness will not be called by such names. Imagine your being called Mr. Briar! You are not a Briar or Mr. Fish; you are not a Fish. These names are worthless to be used as names of human beings.

This is why I mentioned earlier that you must have a Name of Allah (GOD) even to see the hereafter. The Bible teaches you, "Bring every one that is called by His Name" and the words follow that "He Has Created them for His Glory!" Their minds have been changed into His Way of Thinking.

How will the earth be changed? The Bible teaches us that He Will Burn the wicked up and their wisdom will be destroyed by fire and that after one thousand (1,000) years this place will bring forth vegetation, water, and trees. It will be new vegetation, water and trees. It will not be the same as that which we have here today. Do not ask me what kind of vegetation it will be. That is one thousand (1,000) years from now. But I do know that the earth will bring forth new garments of vegetation from this destruction of the world of the wicked.

You say, will you have the make of automobile of Chevrolet, Ford, and Cadillac? No. The people of the new world will not use anything that you see used today in this civilization. The people of the new world will have a superior automobile and planes. They will not be fueled with the same fuel that they use today in this civilization. The fuel that they use today contaminates the air. They speak of the dangerous level of air pollution constantly on the radio and television. Look at the lighting. See how hard it is on the eyes. You will not have this type of light. No. You will have a more soft and clear light than that which is created by the power of electricity.

He makes all things new. He has the Power of heaven and earth. There have been many guesses made of just what type of power will be used in the hereafter. Some guesses have come close and some have not even scratched the surface of that which will come as a new world. You are a long way off in some of the way of thinking and understanding and knowledge of what is yet to come according to what I have been taught by Allah (God) Himself, Who Came in the Person of Master Fard Muhammad, to Whom Praises are due forever.

"For, behold, I create new heavens and a new earth: the former shall not be remembered, or come into mind. " Bible, Is. 65:17.

Here we have a prophecy that Allah (God) Will Make All Things New. "He causes things to grow into a new growth," according to the Holy Qur'an. He Would Not Be a God Who Has Power over all things if He could not Change things according to His Will. If He Could Not Make New People of an old dead people, then He Has Not the Power to Bring In New Things because reproduction is less trouble to do and does not require such a skill as it does to Make something outright new.

Here it refers to both the spiritual and the physical side, but did not He Make us in the Beginning out of nothing?

Look at our creation from sperm to that of a human being. This is a marvelous piece of work of nature which bears witness of the First Creation. We are making new creatures every day. What helps to bring about new creation? When you make a new way of thinking in a person, he is bound to do something new; for he cannot do something other than new since he has a new mind, new ideas. A new mind and new ideas produce a new thing. Just because we have not seen the creation of these things we are quick to disbelieve that they can ever happen.

The Bible, 2 Cor. 5:17 says "Therefore if any man be in Christ, he is a new creature; old things are passed away: behold, all things are become new."

"All who are in Christ is a new creature." This Christ Who is referred to in the above verse is Allah (God) in Person (The Mahdi). This is true and the scripture's prophecy teaches you that You have to be new to be one of His Followers. He changes you in mind; and as it is written "as man think, so is he" (Pr. 23:7).

Christ...the true interpretation of the Name is "The

Crusher." When understood, It makes the God Coming in the Last Day to Crush the wicked to be the True Answer to that Name of Christ. You call Him the Anointed One...That is true. He Is Anointed to Crush the wicked. He does Not Come loving the wicked as you would like Him to do since you are wicked yourself.

The Christians twist the truth of the Bible up in such a way that it will read in their behalf and confound the reader and cause him to think that the devil is also included with the Righteous to reap the Salvation of the Righteous.

As it is written in the Bible, None shall be saved except him who is born of Allah (God)...born of the Nature of Allah (God). In other places of the Bible it is written that "none shall be saved but the pure in heart...the children of the Most High...none but the Righteous."

All of these scriptures prophesy of the type of people whom Allah (God) Will Save. Allah (God) Will Save the people who are born of Allah (God), by nature, the Black Man. We are lucky to be born of Allah (God).

The Black Man thinks in terms that he is just as much hated and despised by Allah (God) as is the white race. The white race is the enemy of Allah (God) by nature. The white race was born and made to be an enemy of Allah (God). The Black Man is not born to be an enemy of Allah (God). That is why Allah (God) Came to Seek us and Save us from that which is rightly due to His and our enemy, (white race). As you find it in the Bible, "He Went Forth to Save and to Deliver His People." The Black People are the people of Allah (God).

The Father of us (Black Man) in the Beginning was

a Black Man and the Father of The Mahdi, The God in the Last Day, is a Black Man. A Black Man is the Father of the Son of Man (The Mahdi).

Black Brother, why should you not believe in your own God Allah, Who Came in the Person of Master Fard Muhammad, to Whom Praises are due forever? He Came to Help you and to Save you from that which is set up for a destruction of another people (white race).

Why should not you, Black Brother, want to be made new since the devil has made you ugly. The devil made you ugly and he tries to keep himself looking good so that he can attract you to follow him to that which you should not go to (the doom of the white man).

Behold He Makes All Things New. Allah (God) Will tear down the false one (white race). How can Allah (God) Build something new and better for us than that which we are living in if He does not first tear the false one down and Build a New house; for the old house has become so disagreeable to live in in peace. We have got to find a better house than this one in which mischief and bloodshed is going on daily. Now we need another house better than this one. Read the Last Book in your Bible, Rev. 2:17. You must have everything new. Read Romans 7:6. These are references of your Bible that you believe in; now you see it verifies the teachings of Islam. Maybe now you will not accept these Bible verifications.

Black Man, I only want you to know that what I am writing is all for your sake so that you may believe. Why should not you believe in your own salvation when everything is in your favor?

As I have pointed out to you in the prophecy that He will make all things new, I have pointed out to you that this includes our being given a new mind which produces new ideas. The new mind and the new ideas are to condition us for the new materialistic things that He will make.

The new people that are to be made are from us (Black Man of America). We will be made a new people, for we have been destroyed mentally and physically by the teachers and guides of this world of the white race. Therefore in order to renew us, (the once servitude slave and the now free slave of our enemy), we must have a new spirit that will produce ideas in us to become a new people. Both the Bible and the Holy Qur'an prophesy that a new generation (people) will be raised up as I have pointed out on the making of a new heaven and a new earth. He can cause a renewal or reproduction of the heavens and the earth — to make it clear, cause them to grow into a new growth. He has the power to do these things. He has not only the Power to bring into existence all the things which we now see present, but He also has the Power to Change that which exists into something else, or to destroy the present existence outright and cause it to waste away outright and bring in a new creation in its place.

You are quick to believe in that which makes no sense at all, but that which makes sense you are not quick to believe in it.

You have been born and reared into spooky beliefs, and you believe that all of the prophecies relating to heaven and the lives of those people are something spooky without form and with no desire to eat or even to drink. You make them formless. The fact is that the way we were taught and brought up instilled these spooky beliefs in our minds. The preachers who preached the Bible did not give to us the understanding of that which was written, but rather they preached as they read it. The reading is to be understood. Could we believe the Bible on face value when it says that Samson killed a lion and then came back and found bees making honey in the carcass and that he ate from it? Could we believe that he would be so foolish as to eat honey out of a dead carcass? No. In the first place it did not mean that he had killed a natural lion. Furthermore, the bee is not so indecent about food for its young that it would seek a carcass to build a home in nor would we be so foolish as to take it for granted that the harlot, Delilah, shaved off the seven (7) locks of Samson's hair or even that his hair was where his strength lay. These writings are to be understood. If we have not the understanding of the words of prophecy which were given to the prophets from Allah (God), then we do not understand the Words of God.

How can such a spiritually blind person believe when he does not understand what he is reading himself? The Jesus was right when he prophesied that the blind cannot lead the blind Mt. 15; 14. This is the classification which he gave to the blind preachers and their blind followers.

Black Preachers who make themselves preachers, although they lack the knowledge of the theology of the Bible, should not be licensed to preach, not to think of ordaining them. But you do so and the white man, who is actually the one who licenses you to preach, backs you up as a Black preacher, knowing that you do not have the knowledge of the scriptures. He did not intend that you have the knowledge of the scriptures. He makes all things new. Who Is He? He is the Son of Man. The Son of Man is made part of both peoples, the Black and the white, so that he may be able to deal with both peoples justly and righteously.

Now here in the Bible is it prophesied that something other than Man is going to do something for man that will better his condition or even to destory his existence...other than another man. Therefore nothing that we see in the animal or fowl world or in water-life on this planet has the power to lead or to guide us. There is none in the other worlds of life who has any interest in us at all. They are not given brains that will think in terms of man or interest in man and his affairs.

He makes all things new. Allah (God) Who Came in the Person of Master Fard Muhammad must make all things new in order to bring in a new government based upon Freedom, Justice, Equality, and Righteousness to displace the world of evil and unrighteousness.

The world of evil and unrighteousness has no base for Allah (God) to Build a world of righteousness upon or to make new heavens or a new earth for the righteous. He must build a new world absolutely from the very bases of righteousness and Justice. Nowhere in this world of the white race are there Freedom, Justice, Equality, and Righteousness. The father of the white race, Yakub, did not put the basis in his race to make a world of Freedom, Justice, Equality, and Righteousness; for the Black Man already has a world of Freedom, Justice and Equality before Yakub made his unrighteous world to oppose our world of righteousness.

The Arab thinks it is something grave to talk about a new Islam. Why certainly, Brother! What have you been going through for the past six thousand (6,000) years under the rule of the devil. Now to reject **The Righteous One** Who not only brings about a new mind and a new idea and a new life and a new change as the

Holy Qur'an teaches you and me today is fatal. It is not that the base of Islam is wrong. I say this time and time again; that the belief in One God, that the Bible and the Holy Qur'an prophesy that you must have, is true. The Belief in one Messenger or shepherd as He is sometimes referred to in the Bible stands true. You will no more have many Gods to believe in, but where both Christian and orthodox Muslim are wrong in that belief, the Christians believe in the return of Jesus to take part in the Resurrection which is contrary to the truth. The orthodox Arab teachers believe that what Muhammad gave is sufficient forever. Certainly it is the truth forever but it does not mean that we should be looking for Muhammad's Holy Qur'an to just take wings and become a man and come among us whom the Holy Qur'an would not prophesy that a new nation, a new generation would be born if that which was received, the Holy Qur'an was sufficient to convert the world. Today the world is more opposed to Islam than ever in a manner of speaking, for the Islamic world is having confusion over the very principles they have been teaching. They have gone so far off the path themselves that they cannot correct or establish a return start for the future of Islam. They must admit that the Holy Qur'an prophesies of the "Coming of Allah (God)" and "The Days of Allah (God)" and what He Can Do. The Holy Qur'an also prophesies that the Messenger and Allah (God) Would Be as One Person, together, and that the Messenger would teach and train his own ministers in that day.

The Muhammad of 1400 years ago. The Muhammad in this prophecy is a man in the Resurrection, for Muhammad of 1400 years ago knew nothing about us in this day and time. We were too far in the future. The prophecy did not prophesy that he would come back to teach us. He cannot teach us.

He could only give us a book to read, an Arabic Holy Qur'an. The Holy Qur'an teaches us that Allah (God) would raise up a Messenger from among the dead, (the so-called Negro), and he must be one given the ministryship to teach them the Way to Allah (God). **He makes all things new.** I say to the world of Islam, **Bow To Him.** The Holy Qur'an teaches us that, "You shall see all nations bowing down to him," Who **Makes All Things New,** Master Fard Muhammad, to Whom Praises are due forever.

Study over the Name Fard; it is sufficient to warn you that this is not the Name that Muhammad prophesies of. In fact Muhammad never saw the God. Muhammad only Heard His Voice. The Muhammad of the prophecy of the Holy Qur'an teaches and prophesies of a Muhammad who would get his Word from the Mouth of Allah (God) and not through visions of talking to Him and never seeing the Speaker. So I say to the Arab world of Islam, prepare yourself for all that you hear coming from the mouth of Messenger Elijah Muhammad here in America. You can accept it or reject it. It Would be good if you accept it. Otherwise you can reject it and meet the fate of those who before you rejected a messenger because of their pride, for they wanted to be that which they were not to be. He makes all things new...

CHAPTER 24

God Helps Those Who Help Themselves!

It is almost unbelievable to see and talk with our people and find in their talk, in this modern rise of advanced education for all, that our very educators and intellectual people desire nothing more than to remain in the "free" mental shackles of slavery with nothing constructive for themselves and their people.

After 400 years (of which one hundred of these years the once-slave masters claim they have freed us), there has not been much of an effort on our part to go free in "deed."

Imagine people out here with B.A., B.S., M.A., M.S., and Ph.D. degrees still begging the white man to give them a job and to care for them as their fathers did in slavery times. This actually shows that the more highly educated and trained our people are, the more they want to be like white people and be recognized as one of them throughout the government of America.

They are leading their poor brothers and sisters in Mississippi, Georgia, Alabama, Florida, the Carolinas, and other southern states as well as the northern states into a more slave-like condition than our parents were in, because this type of slavery (mental slavery) is worse than physical slavery.

If you notice in talking to most intellectual Black people, you can see readily in their conversations that they want to be members in the society of white people. They care not what happens to the poor man in the mud. We could do wonderful things for ourselves if we get the idea of social equality and integrating with white people in their many societies out of our hearts.

Regardless to how disgraceful that society may be (and they have a society now going partly nude), some of our people want to be members of it. Imagine these intellectual people, preachers, and pastors of churches going into spiritual places for the worship of God with their wives and daughters wearing dresses up across their thighs.

What kind of God would recognize you in such a filthy and disrespectful manner of dress in a house called by His Name? God is not a God Who Will recognize respect of filth. He is a Decent and Intelligent God. Your wives and daughters go in a church, sitting, with such styles of dress on, facing the pastor on the speaker's stand and he makes no objection to it whatsoever, but condones it.

We need a Divine Judgment for sure to check and bring to naught the disgrace of God and the worship of Satan (the devil).

Join up with me on the decent and sensible program begining on page 223 of this book. Get business minded; get a creative mind. The degree of education we have today, given to us by the white man, can be used effectively to go for self if we want to go for self.

You do not like doing right. You do not like doing something for self. You glorify begging the white man to do for you that which you can do for yourself. I warn you that the day is not far distant when you will be forced to do something for yourself because the white man is bound to drop you. And that he knows, but he is not telling you. He is allowing you the chance to make a fool of yourself and be caught at that time like a grasshopper who enjoyed summer weather. But cold weather kills the grasshopper. It freezes him to death because he has no house to lodge in.

You do not want to be separated from your enemies regardless of what kind of treatment you receive and they do not want you separated from them, as long as they can hold you with them. You serve as a protection for them and they know you love them and want to be like them. They will agree with you when you say separation will not settle the problem, while that is the main step to take from an enemy who will not do justice by you (leave and go for yourself).

We were not originally born with white people. We have just been among white people four hundred years. So why do you think separation is the answer to your problem with your enemy? God Himself wants to separate from His enemy and you certainly are in the Divine plan to be separated.

You will not even go out of the enemy's house; nor from the front of his gate to do something for yourself that he will allow you to do. We need as a start a hundred million acres of farmland. You say: "No sir! I do not want to farm."

The white man is one of the greatest farmers there is on the earth. America's farms can feed many nations and people — even you and me. Why should not we here, with such industrious people, learn to do the same for ourselves?

You have hundreds of millions of dollars laying in banks here in Chicago and in other banks throughout America. You put your money in the white man's bank for him to use as he pleases. He gives you a little interest on it and you are satisfied.

I proposed establishing a black national bank for ourselves. You cannot see yourself trusting your own

138

self. If you would loan me a few of your millions that you have laying in these banks — not a hundred million, just loan me ten million — I would show you one hundred million dollars for the use of that ten million.

I have to turn to the white man for this loan. He probably will not turn me down because he is tired of taking care of you and having you jumping up in his face and lying down at his gate. He is tired of it, but he does not tell you. He will show you in actions. When he sics his dogs on you, turns his fire hoses on you and kicks you down in the streets, throwing you in his "lock up," he is telling you all the time: "Nigger, get away from my door." But you are like it is written. You take all of this humiliation.

Just think: You have intelligent Black people disgracing themselves, begging the white man to create jobs for them and to accept them as his equal.

Christian preachers, pastors of churches, and other black politicians are caught in this disgraceful begging manner.

In a time when we should be showing the world that after one hundred years up from slavery, we are leading ourselves out of that slavery mentality, put in us by the white slave masters, they are acting worse than our fathers did. Our fathers begged, but they begged to go back to Africa where the white man brought us from.

You give the most ignorant and disgraceful answer, saying that separation will not settle or solve the problem of white people's disrespect of Black people. I say you should suffer his disgrace of you, since he cannot get you to go from him nor will you try and do something for yourself, without him doing it for you.

My followers and I, by the Help of God, and with the

respect of the nations of the earth, are trying to do something for ourselves.

We thank the white man for freeing us. And we shall show him that we are intelligent enough to try now to stay free.

CHAPTER 25

Islam Will Unite Black

Allah (God) has come to unite us. We, the Black People in America, must unite. But Unity only comes on the acceptance of Islam. Without Black Unity, we have no power regardless of how great in numbers we may be.

Divine Wisdom of God is what puts us on the path to ascend to the heights that He Has Vouched for as being safe for us. Allah (God) Has Given to us Islam that we may be successful in the knowledge of self, and the doing for self with His Guidance.

For the first time, Islam, the True Religion of Allah (God) Is Being Offered to us, the Black People in America, by Allah (God) Himself, Who Came in the Person of Master Fard Muhammad, to Whom Praises are due forever. We came from righteousness by nature, but we were deceived by the enemy of righteousness (devil).

As mortar cements and ties brick and stone together into one wall or building, so has Islam come with the love of Black Brother for Black Brother, in order to unite us so that we will become one — one in the power of good and Unity.

In Islam, Allah (God) Offers to take off the Yoke of bondage to satan, the devil, and the chains of slavery and give to us the key that will always be available to us — a key that can keep us out of the prison cells of satan, the devil.

Islam is only entire submission to the Will of God. There are other precepts of Islam that have been made into volumes of books, but the main principle of Islam is for you and me to bow to the Will of God and do His Will.

We have been faithful in bowing to the devil's evil will. But now we must bow to the Will of the God of Truth, Righteousness, and Justice, or be removed from the planet earth.

The light of Truth has come to us in the Person of Master Fard Muhammad, God in Person, to Whom Praises are due forever. It is prophesied in the Bible, Is. 60:1, 2... "Arise and shine, for the light has come." This is the first time that the Light of truth, the knowledge of self, and the knowledge of the enemy of self, and God, Has Been Made Manifest. This is also the first manifestation of the cause of the spiritual darkness that we have lived in for the past six thousand (6,000) years.

The whole world of Black Man which has slept for the past six thousand (6,000) years, under the rule of our enemies (devil white race) needs external washing as well as internal spiritual cleansing. We can find the Black Man living in slum-like conditions throughout the world. To be deprived of the knowledge of self for four hundred (400) years is a long time, but six thousand (6,000) years is even longer.

God referred to this internal and external cleansing in these words, (Mal. 3:3... "He shall sit as a refiner and purifier of silver. He shall purge the priesthood of the people that they may offer unto the Lord an offering in righteousness." Islam comes to reform the so-called Negro and to save him from God's destruction of the enemy devil.

Islam, if carried into practice by you and me, will eradicate all such things as slums because it is people who create slums. When we ask other people to clean up our own filthy houses, we are disgracing our own intelligence and decency.

But the sense of dignity that Islam puts into us forces us to qualify ourselves in intelligence and dignity and to remain qualified. This is the qualification that we need.

Islam qualifies us to return to the Nation of Islam, to which we belong by nature, but from which we were deceived, and brought out of by the devils.

Allah (God) Has Chosen us to Guide us to Himself and to Make of us a nation superior over the present nations — to make us the head, and no longer the tail.

Islam is the Great Wisdom that Allah (God) Promised us through His Prophets. Islam is the Religion of Allah (God) and of the Black Man. Islam is the religion of Jesus and of the prophets before Jesus, and the prophets after Jesus, according to the Bible and the Holy Qur'an.

Allah (God) Could Not Change His Religion, Islam, because one would want to know why He Changed it. Allah (God) Created Himself and He Chose From Himself Islam. Therefore, by nature, He Created Himself, The God Of Islam. Islam has not changed since the Creation. Islam always was. It is our religion and He Will Not accept another religion.

CHAPTER 26

The Will Of Allah Is Being Done

The new world of Islam is coming in — not the old world of Islam, but a new world of Islam. "Behold I make all things new!" Rev. 21:5.

We are living in the change of worlds. The old world is going out and the new world is coming in. This is something to be happy and thankful to Allah for — to bear witness to the change of worlds!

This is the first time that Allah (God) has been known in Person. The coming of Allah in Person indicated this change of worlds — signifying a permanent change, where God will set up His Kingdom of Islam without interference.

This is the end of opposition and attacks against the righteous and their righteous religion, Islam. Islam has a righteous name that corresponds with the principles and beliefs of Islam. It is a very beautiful name.

The white race worked hard for 6,000 years to try to destroy the religion of Allah (God). But the white race missed. We are still here.

The Name, Allah, is a Great Name! I'd rather call Him Allah than to call Him God. God is an English name for the Supreme Being. To say God — this refers to the Supreme Being, but we have too many gods, and we would like to give credit to only One God. So we rather use the name, Allah. I want Allah to have all the credit that we can give to Him!

Allah is a Great Name for the Supreme Being. It means Allah everywhere. It colors everything. I like that Name, Allah!

Let Thy Will be done! The Will of Allah must be done! I want to talk with you a few minutes on the Will of Allah. Let Thy Will be done.

We want always that God do His Will, but we are not always prepared to receive His Will. While we wait for His Will, we do our own will — that is no good!

Thy Will be done! The Will of Allah must be done! We must, today accept the Will of Allah and not our will — not the will of other than Allah.

You have too many gods in your religion, Christianity. We do not know which one you mean. You curse with the Name of God and you are always disrespectful to the honor due to that Name.

Allah says there is no God but He. Allah Is the Best Knower. If you want to make a spook out of me, look at me, good, — I am not a spook. I stayed with Allah and we were together for three years and and four months, night and day. If you think you know Allah, better, here I am —question me.

The Will of Allah must be done. Allah, through His Will, will come out Himself to be the champion and lead the righteous to Victory. His Will shall not be hindered by anyone.

When a person gets righteous, God accepts him as His FRIEND. Then the will of each other is with each is with each other. What one wills, the other wills. It is the will of both.

The Messenger's will is in accord with the Will of Allah. The Messenger cannot will something opposed to Allah. Allah has taken over the Messenger's heart, mind, and brain and Allah is making them to react according to His Will!

This is what the Holy Qur'an teaches — that the Will of Allah is the will of the Messenger and the will of the Messenger is the Will of Allah.

Jesus himself said that he was not God. The coming of Jesus was not God. The coming of Jesus was not ever prophesied in the Old Testament of the Bible. What you read of Jesus, in the Old Testament—that is myself: the last days with a government upon his shoulder. Isa. 9:6. Jesus did not have a government upon his shoulder, which is what he needed for a prophet that is to rule, attack, and destroy the Jews, Christians, and Greeks—authorities over religion. He needed that knowledge and power. If he had a government upon his shoulder—what government?

The Will of Allah must be done! Knowledge and belief are different. I can believe that there is an airplane out there on the doorstep, but there is no airplane out there.

There are many people who believe that angels are out in the air somewhere, but if they are out there, we cannot see them. There is no such thing as formless spirits flying around out there somewhere in space, unless it is righteous minds.

The Will of Allah must be done. Allah could not have a Will Himself until He had brains, Himself. Allah was created; self-created from an atom of life. The atom of life was not only able to create flesh and have blood from the earth that He was created on—Allah (God) was created on the very earth that we are on today. But the earth was not as it is today.

I want to come back to our subject, our text, the Will of God. The Will of Allah must be done. Allah's (God's) Will could not be done as long as He has an enemy powerful enough to force his rule against the Will of God.

Allah (God) allowed the enemy 6,000 years in which to rule. Now this is the time that the enemy cannot force his will against the Will of Allah. The white man no longer has power to force his will against Allah and against the representatives of Allah, the prophets!

Thy Will be done. The Will of Allah must be done. It is not the Will of Allah that His people, the Black People, be sick. When a man has no sickness in his body, we call him happy. He is happy. He does not feel any pain; the body is happy.

This is just the life Allah (God) teaches you to enjoy. It is not the will of Allah that you get sick. You make yourself sick.

Allah does not have a set time for you and me to die. We kill ourselves. We can prolong our lives by living right and eating the right food.

People who want their will to be done, let them go to Allah and obey Allah and the Messenger.

CHAPTER 27

Friendship Of Allah (God)

Of all friendships of friends and relations, there is no friendship that is equal to the Friendship of Allah (God). To have Allah (God) as our Friend, we have a Place of Refuge — we have a shelter from the great stormy tempest of the wicked.

The Friendship Of Allah (God) is the kind of Friendship and Refuge that the Black Man in America should seek. We, the Muslims who have submitted ourselves to the Will of Allah (God), do His Will so that Allah (God) May Be Pleased to Do For us and To Be our Friend.

Within the scope of four hundred (400) years we have not had a friend here in America. If the white man says that we are from the jungles of Africa, then we say the reptiles, the beasts, and the other wild life of the jungle are better friends to us than the civilized white slavemakers.

Now To Have The Supreme Being as our Friend and to have Him Befriend us — we could not hope for a better friend. He is worth all other friends combined.

Concerning Faith in Allah (God), the Bible teaches you and me that Allah (God) met Abraham and upon submission he was able to get the honor of being the friend of God because Abraham submitted to the Will of Allah (God). The history of Abraham is the history of all of the righteous who submit to do the Will of Allah (God) — they are successful.

From Noah to Muhammad, the righteous have triumphed over their enemies. We, the Black Man in America, are so foolish that we want to take an open enemy to be our friend instead of Allah (God) Himself.

The White race has never shown true friendship to us. When they are planning to do evil against us they offer us a false show of friendship.

The Great work that I am doing in your midst, in the Name of Him Who Has Taught Me and Who Guides Me to Do His Will, should be enough for you to know that we have Allah (God) Who Came in the Person of Master Fard Muhammad for our Friend.

I am so happy to know that I have a Friend in Allah (God). Never before in all of my life could I say that I had a friend. The Friendship of Allah (God) is the kind of Friendship that we all should have.

Regardless to how many there are of us here on Western soil or in the Western Hemisphere, we should all seek Allah (God) Who Came in the Person of Master Fard Muhammad, to Whom Praises are Due forever, for Friendship.

Some Of Us, being ignorant and proud of ourselves under the false friendship of the devil, think that we are secure under the devil's false power. There is the noise of the thunder of war clashing over the whole world of mankind and it has touched the home of the original man as well. Everybody is fighting for survival. But as I have preached to you for nearly forty years, the population of your and my Black people, our Black Nation, reaches into the billions instead of into the thousands.

The Muslim has not only the Friendship of Allah (God), but the Muslim has the friendship of all Black, Brown, Yellow, Red or whatever color people there may be other than the white people. You know and you have seen it printed in Black and white how the world of our People regardless to their color (except the white man), when it comes to the Muslims, they are our friends. This is due to Allah's Love and Friendship for us who accept the Islamic Faith which is the religion of Abraham and the prophets. Islam is entire submission to the Will of Allah (God) Who Came in the person of Master Fard Muhammad to Whom Praises are Due forever.

We, the Black Man in America, have nothing — no money and no decent homes to live in. Allah (God) Is The Giver, and to reject the offer of The Friendship of Allah (God) Who Came in the Person of Master Fard Muhammad, to Whom Praises are Due forever, to better our condition and set us in heaven at once—for our rejection, our flesh should fry in hellfire.

I think that there are many meaningful Black professional people who could, if they would, unite with me and my Followers and the whole picture of America would change at once.

With the Help of Allah (God), we will not fail. Allah (God) Will Not Let us fail. But we need the sure Friendship of a friend that will not fail us in the time of trouble. For this is the time of trouble in which we are living.

Do Not look for the Judgment to come. You are in the Judgment now. The 'Day of Judgment' means the 'Years of Judgment'. The 'Day' referred to does not mean "a twenty-four (24) hour day". The Holy Qur'an refers to the 'Judgment as the 'Days of Allah (God).' The expression 'years' is used to refer to days and 'days' refers to years.

But those days are expired now, and America is number one on Allah's (God's) List of countries for Him to Deal with. America is first because of her evil done and the evil which she continued to do to her Black once-slave.

We must remember that the scriptures prophesy (Bible Rev.) that in one day death and mourning came to her (America). That day is not far distant. The people are so confused here in America that there is no agreement nor trust in each other.

Believe and Obey me. And if you love Allah (God), He Will Love you. He Will Be your Friend and Protect you from the evil planning of this evil world; for they plan the destruction of the Black slave. It seems as though they should love the Black once - slave since the Black slave has done so much and has suffered untold misery from the hand of his white slave-master who has been so loyal in helping the white slave-master fight to the death in all of his wars for the sake of the white slavemaster.

This is the day that the white slave-master continues to kill you and me as though the Black slave has once robbed the white man of his country; and so he wants to get even with the Black slave.

But as it is written, "As she (America) has done, so shall it be done unto her."

Take Allah (God) for your Friend, Black Man, for Allah (God) is a Sure Friend.

151

CHAPTER 28

Christianity Versus Islam

Examining the truth of the two religions, Islam and Christianity the basic beliefs in Christianity are:

1. God is the Father;
2. Jesus is His son, and
3. The Holy Ghost; and these three are one God.

Note: Adam is supposed to have been the first man that God created, but he is never referred to as the son or as a begotten or only son.

There is one thing I hope to make clear to my people and that is: the Christian religion, as taught and misunderstood by them, is not what they have thought it was. Jesus' history refers more to a future Jesus than the past. There is a prophecy of a Son being prepared to redeem man (the so-called Negroes). This Jesus made His appearance July 4, 1930 and His work is now in effect.

Jesus (Isa) of 2,000 years ago cannot do us any good nor harm. It is outright ignorance to believe that He can. We should be intelligent enough to believe in that which can be or has been proven true. Making the Son and the Holy Ghost the equal with the Father is absolutely sinful. There is no proof that there was or ever shall be a time when people will return to life after they are physically dead. There is no proof that God was the father of Mary's son, nore is ther proof that He is alive some place waiting to return for the Judgment.

The Holy Qur'an says: "And they say: 'The Beneficent God has taken to Himself a Son.' "

Certainly you have made an abominable assertion. The heavens may almost be rent thereat, and the earth cleave asunder; and the mountains fall down in pieces that they ascribe a son to the Beneficent God. And it is not worthy of the Beneficent God that He should take to Himself a son" (19:88-92). God is self-sufficent. He does not need a son to help Him with the people. "What do then those who disbelieve (the Christians) think that they can take My servants to be guardians besides Me? Surely we have prepared hell for the entertainment of the unbelievers" (18:102).

The Christians who are guilty of disbelieving in Allah and His religion, Islam, and who charge God with getting a son by Mary and here warned that Allah has prepared hell for them. You should question the teachers and their teachings of any religion. Take no religion without the knowledge of its truth, lest you be made a fool.

Jesus did not make himself the equal of God. The Holy Qur'an says: "Jesus said: 'Surely I am a servant of Allah; He has given to me the Book and me a prophet (not His son) and He has made me blessed wherever I may be, and He has enjoined on me prayer and poor-rate so long as I live!' " (19:30-31). We cannot find anything to give Jesus as a title but a "prophet" and He did prophesy. BUT as the holy Qur'an further says: "But parties from among them (the Christians) differed, so woe to those who disbelieve, because of their presence on a grievous day" (19:37). There just is no defense for such false teachings as the religion of Christianity. Who can say, with truth, that they have seen the Jesus in flesh and blood after his death? Who can say, with truth, that the Holy Ghost or spirit is the equal to its producer?

The very emblem of CHRISTIANITY IS

disgraceful to the righteous: a cross and the image of a man nailed thereon with a crown of thorns on his head and a wound in his heart. Such signs the so-called Negroes should never look at and they should hate and abominate the one who offers them such ghastly and shameful emblems. Most times the crucified figure is nude except for a strip of cloth over his private parts.

This is the very way that they lynch so-called Negroes; mutilating their bodies and then offering you a piece of the rope that the man was hung with as a warning to you that you will be next. They burn the cross as warnings to you even though the cross, they claim, is sacred among their religious believers.

I say with almost tears in my eyes: brothers and sisters give up believing in such a religion and join on to the religion (Islam) of our father, Abraham, and take for yourself the crescent for your emblem which is universally recognized.

The truth has arrived for us, the lost-found members of the darker people of earth here in America, to stop playing the "fool" among ourselves and the world of mankind and make up our minds whether we are going to hold on to that religion which the white race teaches us or believe in the kingdom of the God of our people which is taught by our people.

We make fools of ourselves to please our enemies (the white race). The average so-called Negro in America is not concerned about love and unity among his own kind but is really interested in trying to get love and unity among other than his own kind.

Of all the histories of people upon our planet earth, past and present, we can find no people who have loved their enemies and hated themselves but the American so - called Negroes. They love and admire their enemies and all that goes for their enemies. They are ready in an instant to dispute, oppose, and kill you if you are not likewise.

I am a lover of my own people and a hater, like God, of all our enemies and I fear only God who has raised me up from among my people to bring them out of the darkness of falsehood into His right of truth so that they may enjoy heaven while they live. There are but a very few so-called Negroes who have spent any time examining the truth of the Bible and the white man's Christianity. Therefore, they are without the real truth of the Bible and Christianity. I know the consequence of trying to bring truth to our people who are in love with those who have taken their fathers out of truth into falsehood. But my life and my death are for this cause.

If we are to accept a religion that is said to be from God, we should diligently examine the truth and the author of that religion, its people, and the contents of its book or books before we bear witness that it is the truth from God and the right religion. Let the so-called Negroes take a second look at the Bible; every word which white Christians want Black men to believe in from God. There is no mention of a religion by the name of Christianity from God or the prophets. Again we must remember that God does not represent Himself to us in the opening or closing of the Bible. He is represented by someone other than Himself.

There His creation is pointed out to us as a proof that there is a Supreme Being over all this universe and that it was made in six days (Genesis 1:1-31) God does not address Himself to us throughout the first chapter. Not His religion nor even the name of the representation of God is mentioned there.

This reader is without authentic proof of just who is

the author of the book called Genesis. You must remember that from the King James authorized version of the Bible, it has been only 346 years and you have only been permitted to read the Bible for the past 90 years. The white man, our slavemaster and enemy, had the Bible over 250 years before we were allowed to read the book.

Now you seem to know more about the purity of the Bible than those who translated it into their own language. Not only do you try defending the Bible as being the word of God, but you try equally to defend the white race and their wicked world.

You must remember and never forget that the white Christian race made slaves of our fathers and will not allow you now to rise above the status of a free slave! Why is the Pope, who lives in Rome, Italy, the head of the Christian churches when Jesus was born in Palestine and did the greater portion of His teachings in and around Jerusalem? Why is not Jerusalem the capital and head of the Christian churches? We (the Muslims) took Jerusalem and the tomb of Jesus in 1187 A.D.

Certainly there is a Saviour predicted for you, but not the one of two thousand years ago, but the one that Jesus prophesied would come after Him who will redeem us from the hands of our enemies.

CHAPTER 29

Mary, Joseph, and Jesus

The 25th of December is the birthday of Nimrod, the evil demon of the white race, who was born in the last 300 years of the civilization of Moses (17th Century B.C.).

From Moses to Jesus, there were many minor prophets and there were many wicked rulers. Jesus came, warning the white race that if they did not accept the truth of their coming doom, it would come to them in a day that they would not be aware of.

The deceitful theologians and writers of Christianity along with their chief, the Pope of Rome, know the truth; but yet have deceived the people as to the knowledge of the truth by deceiving them to worship an evil demon like Nimrod. They have the history of Nimrod with them and they use him under the name of Jesus to deceive the people to make them believe that the 25th of December was Jesus' birthday. And, in this way, they would have the world worshipping this wicked evil demon, Nimrod, for the all but perfect prophet, Jesus.

But Jesus was not born in December. God in the Person of Master Fard Muhammad, to Whom Praises are due forever, has taught me that his birthday took place between the first and second weeks of September, and that no one knows exactly what day he was born, for it was a secret kept between Joseph and Mary to save them both from being murdered by getting a baby out of wedlock.

The real truth that the Christians hate to confess is

that Joseph had gotten the child, Jesus, by Mary while he was married to another woman and at that time had six children by the first marriage. So Master Fard Muhammad (God in Person) has taught me.

The Christians portray Joseph as someone taking care of a pregnant woman while he had nothing to do with the pregnancy of Mary. But let us think sanely, as the Bible teaches us that Mary was put in the care of Joseph.

How could the theologians of the Bible write that the woman met Joseph to assure him that he does not not have to fear taking Mary into marriage for that which she is pregnant with is not from man; it is from God, the Holy Ghost?

And, how could Joseph accept such an excuse for Mary's pregnancy when he had not the knowledge of any woman in the history of man being found pregnant with a Holy Ghost's son? For ghost means something that does not exist.

Instead, the theologians who wrote the history of Jesus and Mary should have used such words as: The child that Mary is pregnant with is a Holy child or a Prophet and you, Joseph, are the father of this Prophet and you should not fear accepting her and accepting the truth that you are the father of the child that Mary is pregnant with because the child will be the last Prophet to the white race (Jews). This would have made sense. Allah, in the Person of Master Fard Muhammad, To Whom Praises are Due forever, had taught me that this woman, whom the Bible mentions, told Joseph to his face that he was the father of the child that she was pregnant with and not the false teachings of the Bible that Jesus was something of a Holy Ghost and not flesh and blood.

The theologians got this from the Jews who also

158

accused Joseph of being the father of the child and that he made Mary pregnant by visting her under the cover of darkness (the Jews charged him with acting like a ghost and visiting her under the cover of darkness and making Mary pregnant).

Joseph and Mary had promised to marry when they were going to school at the age of 6 and they were separated. Since Joseph was a poor man and Mary's father was a rich man, he refused to give Mary over to Joseph when he became a man and Joseph went and married another woman and had been married to her for six years and had six children by this wife. When the opportunity came that he could visit Mary (as she called him and told him of the opportunity), he made good of it.

Then the love they had for each other when they were little sprang anew again while they were alone together in the absence of Mary's father and this act took place. So Allah, in the Person of Master Fard Muhammad, to Whom Praises are Due forever, taught me.

CHAPTER 30

"And We Made The Son Of Mary And His Mother A Sign, And We Gave Them Refuge On A Lofty Ground Having Meadows And Springs."

If the Bible students would have taken this 50th verse of the 23rd Chapter of the Holy Qur'an, under study together with the birth, ministry and death of Jesus, as given in the Bible, Matt., Mark, Luke and John, they would agree that the man, Jesus, 2,000 years ago and his mother were a sign of something to come.

But the preachers of Christianity have always been overly anxious to put some fancy myth (other than the truth) around Jesus' birth, ministry, and death, 2,000 years ago, to the extent that the Catholics make monuments of an imaginary Mary and her son, Jesus, and bow down and worship their handmade statues.

The Christians have no true pictures of Jesus and his mother, Mary, in possession, so they use imagery and the ignorant take it for truth.

The son of Mary and his mother, a sign. Let us see if we can direct the sign and find something that corresponds with her son's birth and the hostile attitude of the Jews against the prosperity and future of these two people.

Why was the government, at that time, against the birth of Jesus and his freedom to live as other men?

The Bible, Matt. 2:8, teaches that on his birth, when Herod heard of it, sent spies to ascertain the truth of the news that Mary had given birth to a child called Jesus. He told them to bring word to him that he may go and worship him. But by no means did he intend to give a true worship and recognition of Mary's son, Jesus. He desired death for the son because he had read the Torah and in it is a prophecy of the Coming and Birth of a Ruler who would be King of the Jews. He felt that his authorities and rule would be threatened and brought to a naught if this was the baby prophesied of.

Take this anger and dislike on the part of the beast that seeks to destroy the child of a woman, Bible, Rev. 12:4 "...and the dragon stood before the woman which was ready to be delivered, for to devour her child as soon as it was born." If Mary and her son are a sign, or an example, of that which is to come, then whose birth and enslavement could correspond with these prophecies and signs any more than we, the American So-Called Negroes here under the white man?

Our god is nursing us into the knowledge of our Black self, as a mother nurses her babies from a nursing bottle or from her breasts. The angry enemy watches the growth of the children whom God Has Chosen to build for Himself a kingdom. The enemy becomes angrier and angrier as the American so - called Negro (the Lost - Found Members of the Aboriginal Nation) grow into the knowledge of self, our God and our True Religion, Islam (Entire submission to the Will of God).

In the Bible, the Book of Revelation gives a symbolic picture of the story of Mary and her son, Jesus, which is recounted in the 1st Chapter of Matt., but nevertheless, if understood, it is easy to see that Mary and her son were a sign of the American so-called Negro coming in the future. He would have a worse enemy against him; one who has the nature of a beast.

As Herod did, the enemy admires the so - called Negro, but at the same time he hopes to trick the Negro to go down with him to his doom. As it is prophesied, Bible Rev. 19:20, actually the beast did deceive the people.

The Prophets say that the slave, being deceived, worshipped the mark of the slave-master (his religion and name). There are many of our people today who hope to be dignified and respected by worshipping the cross and by going in the slave-master's name.

This worship called Christianity and the names of the white slavemaster dooms Black Americans to an eternal death in the fire of hell. This fire of hell will be kindled from the atmosphere and sun over America. This is the only part of the earth of which it is prophesied that God would turn it into a Lake of Fire; not the whole earth. The reason it is called a lake is because a lake is confined to a certain area. A lake is inland surrounded by land.

The fleeing of Mary with her son to Egypt and Joseph's aiding her to make haste to Egypt Bible Matt. 2:13, is a beautiful sign of the so-called American Negro fleeing out of America to the open arms of the Muslim world.

The King, Herod, desired most of all to kill Jesus in his infancy. Bible, Rev. 12:4 tells us that the dragon stood before the woman. The woman here represents the Messenger of God. The child represents the followers of the Messenger.

In the Bible, Rev. 14:1, we find the Lamb (Messenger of Allah, God) standing on the Mount Zion (foreign shore); with him was a hundred and forty four thousand (his followers who had escaped from the anger of the beast).

The average so-called Negro preacher has always believed this was referring to Jesus, the son of Mary. But this is due to his lack of knowledge of the Bible story of Jesus. Jesus, as I have said and written, was only a prophet. He is not what the average so-called Negro is made to believe from the surface teachings of the Bible. They have been taught that Jesus is some kind of mysterious being, and not a natural man, and that he is God, and that he could be killed, put into a grave back there 2,000 years ago, and ascend up into space to await the end of the world. They have been taught to believe that he will return and usher in the Judgment of this world. All of this is wrong.

The fleeing out of Jerusalem under the cover of darkness is backed up by prophecy made in the Bible, Ez. 34:12, "...and will deliver them out of all places where they have been scattered in the cloudy and dark day." This is referring to the last days; that Allah (God) would gather us in under a cover of a cloudy and dark day. We go further back to prophecy. Bible Ex. 12:31, 42 says that Israel was brought out of Egypt under cover of darkness. The Bible, Rev. 8:12 refers to a time of darkness in which "the third part of the sun, moon and stars was smitten and it was dark part of the day and the night."

Since the world that Allah (God) will be destroying is a world of spiritual darkness, it is natural then that his judgment should correspond with the spiritual darkness of the evil world that He is removing.

In the Bible, Rev. 16:3, the angel dropped a vial into the sea, and the sea was turned to blood. The angel who had the power to do this work said that this was good as they loved the drawing of blood, they were given blood to drink. This refers to their evil murdering of people, especially the Black Man. No one fits this description better than America. She thought there was no help for us. But help has come to us as the Bible, Is. 62:4, prophesies, "Thou shalt no more be termed Forsaken..."

Retaliation is certain today, for Allah (God) has chosen us to be His People. Our enemy is angry against God Coming to our aid and His Raising of us into a true knowledge of self, Our God, and His True Religion, the same as Herod and the beast of Revelation (Bible) was against Jesus and the woman who was giving birth to her child.

The white man hates to see anything of good come to the American so-called Negro whom he has made blind, deaf, and dumb to the knowledge of self and others. He is working feverishly to bring to a naught the progress of the salvation that Allah (God), Who Came in the Person of Master Fard Muhammad To Whom Praises are due forever, has brought to us, the Black Man of America.

As Joseph was at his wits' end trying to find a place for Jesus and His mother, Mary, at the time of his birth, (Bible Lk. 2:7) so are we. Everywhere that we go trying to find an Inn to give birth to this baby (so-called American Negro) we are hindered, not by the common people but by the chief rulers of this land.

CHAPTER 31

The Christian Holidays

My Dear Black Brothers and Black Sisters, the religion Christian holidays that you celebrate are holidays for white people and not for Black People.

The white people do not worship any day belonging to Black People. Why should you worship their days... days which are to their interest and not to the interest of the Black Man?

On the 25th day of December, when you seek to worship the birthday of Jesus, you are just as far from worshipping his birthday, as two thousand (2,000) years ago is to this past September. For Jesus was not born in December.

Allah (God) Who Came in the Person of Master Fard Muhammad, to whom Praises are due forever, Taught me that Jesus was born between the first and second week in September. If any Christian thinks that Allah (God) Is Misleading you and me, let the theologians of Christianity attack His Word and show proof that they are worshipping Jesus' birthday on the 25th day of December and that Jesus of 2,000 years ago rose from his grave on that day they celebrate as Easter.

As a People who have been robbed and spoiled as we the Black People have been robbed of our own, naturally we dance by the music of the white slave - master and his children until we learn who we are.

So now we are learning who we are and a great separation is taking place between Black and white. We cannot hinder this separation even if we try to do so because it was Divinely Appointed thousands of years ago that a separation between good and evil would come about.

We, the Black People are from the God of Good; we are not from the god of evil. This, I repeatedly teach you. And the world of religious scientists will bear me witness, because this is true.

We make a fool out of ourselves by jumping up worshipping days and people that the white slave - master and his children say we are to worship.

We, the Black People, have no right to worship one day of Jesus of two thousand (2,000) years ago; for Jesus came ahead of time to bring about a judgment of this people and he died for the mistake that he had made in understanding the scripture. Then Jesus declared that he would go away... give his life... for what he had stood for.

So you do not have anything to worship on any day of the year for Jesus because he did not have any day for us to worship. If he had had a day to be worshipped on, it would have been for Jews and not for you and me, for we were not there to be represented.

Jesus came to the Jews and not to us and then he got disappointed that he was ahead of the time of the Jews to preach the doctrine of the destruction or judgment and the setting up of a New Kingdom of Heaven after the destruction of the Jew's civilization. Jesus was born two thousand years ahead of the judgment of the Jews.

So you go out and spend your hard - earned money to worship with white people. They force you under disguise and defraud you into worshipping the birthday of that wicked old Nimrod on December And if you knew the truth of him, you would not dare to worship it.

And so many false statements have been made to

keep the falsehood strong enough for you to continue to believe until today; falsehood has come face to face with truth. And falsehood cannot stand in the face of truth. Truth condemns falsehood.

This world and this life and this way of civilization is falling and it soon will be no more. You are at the end of it before you realize it. Of course the scientists of the white people try to tell you, but, you are so sold to the falsehood that they have taught you and me for the last four hundred (400) years that you have come to love it. You would rather have the false than to have the truth. That is why you do not follow me.

But everyone of you should take those bells off your door. It is a foolish thing to worship a God with a bell, while the Bible tells you that God will use a trumpet. If you display anything, it should be a trumpet and not a bell to announce the Resurrection and Judgment.

Leave off the false; for truth has come and falsehood must vanish.

CHAPTER 32

Whose Christmas?

If You look at the emblems which represent these two religions and understand their meanings, you will say, "How could I have ever been a Christian? Or ever to have believed in such a religion which will display such a gruesome sign—a murdered prophet to beckon me on a path to murder."

The whole history of the white race is written in the shedding of innocent blood. They kill the righteous. Do you not hear how openly they speak of killing me and my followers? Do you not see how they go in gangs, armed to the teeth, to kill me and my followers? They try to provoke us to strike back at them — innocent people upon whom they prey.

They attack our meeting places like wild jungle creatures; actually shoot up the walls of our temples to show their hatred of the righteous and the right - doer — without any cause whatsoever, as you see and know. We carry no weapons, but this is no defense or excuse to the white race, which is, by nature, made to attack and kill the innocent without an excuse.

They go in carloads and truckloads, raiding the poor innocent Black sections to take our lives without any cause or provocation whatsoever — wrecking our property — knowing that we have no arms. They cowardly, evilly come in great numbers as though they expect a great army to rise up against them. Cowards!

They have no respect for good. They bomb our Black Christian brothers' churches in the South. They Shoot them down on highways, in their homes and on the job—anywhere he can satisfy his lust for blood; a blood-thirsty wicked human beast.

They go out on the streets and run down the poor Black man to take his life, with no excuse except their hatred of him and to bear witness to the truth of himself that he is the devil.

They have the nerve to tell the poor innocent victim (Black man) that the teacher of the truth is teaching hatred of him! Who could love him? There should be no need to teach hatred of you to a people who were born and brought up under your feet and who daily experience the cruel blows from your heavy boots, because that person already knows that you are the heartless enemy—who will not let him go free in a separate place here in this wide territory.

But You would rather hold them here under your eyes so that you can do evil things to them — beat and kill them while they are helpless. Your enemies would gladly arm every one of them, but Allah (God) does not want us to bear arms.

He wants to show you that he is God. He wants to fight you with His weapons, the forces of nature — rain, hail, snow, and earthquakes; the sun, moon, and the star. As little as we respect that little dried up piece of our planet called moon, which looks harmless, it has such power of magnetic pull on our planet that it could affect our lives.

Now comes the Christians' big holiday which they call Christmas. With all the fantastic foolishness of jungle savages, they pretend to love worshipping the prophet on the 25th day of December. They stagger drunkenly all over the streets, campuses, and most of the homes and churches, with card games, dice and other games of chance and all kinds of whisky and beer — to celebrate that great prophet; with fighting and killing and eating swine flesh. Such is the day which they call the birthday of Jesus.

They have nothing of good in their behavior. It is like Isaiah said, "This people worship me with their mouth but their hearts are far from me." This is true.

It is all false that Jesus was born on the 25th day of December. But the poor Black slave, who used to rejoice that his master gave him one day of rest from the hard labor which he was made to serve, until any day his master said was a holiday was all right with him, as long as he did not have to work.

Until this day, they do not stop to ask what is the meaning of his holiday and where it sprang from. There is no holiday of the white people which the so-called Negro should worship as his day. He never seeks to find a day of his own on which he can worship.

He seeks to worship what the white man worships — and feels rejected if not permitted to go to war with his master regardless of whom his master is fighting, even though it be his own brother or family. He thinks he is disgraced if he is not involved in whatsoever his master is involved in, and he believes he has a share in it because he wants the love and respect of his master so much.

In fact, He does not believe in what he teaches you of Christianity. Even the very basic principle of Christianity is wrong and false (three Gods in one). And that one of them had to die, He being the Son of the Father, to save the wicked world of the Caucasian race is the most damnable teaching against your peace and happiness. It takes you right out of life.

Another false practice on the 25th day of December: the children between the ages of 3 and 12 think a Santa Claus is visiting them, making them believe they are getting presents from some foreign or strange person other than themselves (the parents).

170

Some of the parents go so far as to scratch the chimney and tell the children "Santa came down here last night." This is outright false and telling other than the truth. They even have pictures made and commercialized on it.

How could one come from way around the North Pole driving a small sled-like cart? And where did he buy all of those toys? How does Santa drive his sled in the South where there is no snow or ice for him to drive on? They rob themselves of the honor of the child at his receiving their gifts.

Jesus is garbed up and commercialized on by a world of evil and sin and you like this, my people—you love this now. You defy anyone, even God Himself, to try and remove your love of what is false.

You cannot prove that the 25th day of December is the birthday of Jesus and you are preaching out of a Bible which does not carry any such history. It gives you an idea that He could not have been born on December 25 by these words "While the shepherd watched their flocks by night."

If it had been in December, could they have been sitting out at night watching the flock eat good green grass? December is wintertime! Winter starts on the 21st day of December—you are four days into winter there.

Of course, there are some parts of the earth where winter does not come and there is pasture for the sheep all year round. But it is not like that in Palestine — in the winter, especially at night.

According to the Christian saying and representation, the Son of God is worshipped. His birth is mocked and disgraced with drunkeness, murdering, gambling, and every type of evil committed on such a day by the Christians while the Muslims walk through their midst, soberly, peacefully fasting through the month and not thinking or drinking alcoholic beverages — not eating the flesh of anything —eating once a day, and that only at night.

At the same time, the evil Christian world disgraces the name of one of the most perfect prophets of the past, Jesus. Should not God take revenge on them for such mockery of Jesus? They lie when they say Jesus was born without the agency of man. Then they lie of his death and say that he rose again physically.

And yet, the Black preacher today, in this modern, advanced spiritually scientific world which represents such falsehood, scorn the truth of Islam (entire submission to the Will of God). Should not the preacher be divinely chastised as it is written that he will be?

The Pope of Rome knows that his followers here in the West are making a mockery of Jesus and his teachings, but he will not try to change it, for he is the father of it (church).

The Sign Of Christianity is death. The sign of Islam is life. Teach your children the truth. Make them practice truth. Make them practice truth, and do so yourself, as their guides.

CHAPTER 33

Christmas!

On the 25th day of December comes another Christian holiday that they say is observed in remembrance of Jesus. Some say it is to keep in remembrance of his birth date. The late writers, on the word Christmas, seem to be ashamed to go along with the old writers that the 25th day of December was the birth date of Jesus because there has been so much research on whether or not Jesus was even born in December. But since it is a Christian holiday, they are not particular whether or not Jesus or the Roman Caesar was born on that day; for the real good of holidays by the Christians is to commercialize on the public.

They sell much merchandise of various kinds, even now to automobiles, maybe airplanes, and boats. Suits of clothes are some of the main items of merchandise that are sold plentifully around Christmas — shoes, new pieces of furniture in the home, and other home decorations.

The merchants' pockets are made fat for Christmas — the tobacco factories, the beer and whisky traffic, and wine. These three things, beer, wine, and whisky, find a great sale at Christmas time. Also much wild game is bought. And the fattest pig that their farmer can produce is bought. All of these things, especially intoxicating liquors and the eating of swine flesh and drunkenness, dancing, and gambling, are done on the day that they commemorate for a man that they claim to have been a most perfect man; holy, righteous, the son of God. There is no holy worship on that day for him. The government of Christianity throws open the freedom of worship at that time (Christmas) to both savages, clergymen, and Christian sages (the wise) to disgrace the prophet of God whom they, themselves exalted to the point of being God Himself.

What a world of Christianity. Now comes the date and birth of Jesus which no one knows. Allah (God) in the Person of Master Fard Muhammad, to Whom Praises are due forever, taught me that since Jesus' birth was expected by his enemies, the date and place (especially the date) was kept as a secret between Mary and Joseph, the father and mother of Jesus, to keep the authorities from killing him; for the Jews had learned from their scripture that he was their last Prophet and that he would curse them because of their unbelief and destroy their independence among their brethren (the white race). God said to me that the Jesus, who is so much talked about in the Christian circles, was born in the first or second week of September — not on the 25th of December — that the famous Nimrod, who broke Moses civilization by 300 years, was born on the 25th day of December.

Here come us, the American Black people, who were kept blind, deaf and dumb to the reading of the Bible for 300 years; arguing and disputing on the birth of Jesus, saying that Jesus was born on the 25th day of December.

Whatever he has learned from his master (white race), he is willing to die on it (that it is the truth); while he does not even know the truth of himself. They take the Bible as it reads; they know not its meanings at all. And they will scorn the meanings of it by one of them whose meanings have been taught to him by

God Almighty — that the scripture may be fulfilled; that He would send a teacher or preacher to us, the Lost and Found people; and raise him up from among us. Abraham and his son, Ishmael, according to the Qur'an, also prayed to Allah (God) that He might raise up an apostle from among the Lost - Found and mentally dead people and to teach him the knowledge of the Book (Bible) and the Wisdom (Holy Qur'an) that he may teach others of his people the meanings of what they read out of the Bible and Qur'an.

But what does this do to the rest of the people? It causes them to become jealous and envious of that tone whom God confers more of His Divine knowledge upon than He does the rest. This is what is happening right at this very hour. The Holy Qur'an plainly teaches us that every one of us wanted the same thing that He gave the Messenger. That is the knowledge of the Book and the Wisdom of God and the Qur'an. It is prophesied that the Lost Found Black Man would envy the knowledge that God would bestow upon his servant — to teach them the knowledge of that which before they knew not.

This is the American So-Called Negro. The Bible teaches that they all wanted to be shepherds therefore the sheep went astray. What a jealous and envious people the Black people are.

This is why we can be divided so easily against each other. It is because the devils soon see that none wants to follow the other.

Look how they are reaching out at what I am teaching, placing it on their "coat lapels" and in their books, and mixing it up with their own corrupted ideas; just to be called leaders.

Not only has Christianity deceived the people by falsifying the birthday of Jesus; they have shown themselves as evil worshippers of righteousness by the way they celebrate this day they call the birthday of Jesus (25th day of December). The greatest drunken day in the whole year of 365 days you see on the 25th day of December; fighting and murdering each other.

The week before this day (25th of December), the righteous are afraid almost to walk among the worshippers of Christmas.

To call it Christ Mass (a mass of people meeting to worship one of Allah's Divine Messengers and the last one to the Jews) is wrong because Christ was not born on that day two thousand years ago. Christ was born in 1877. Christ, according to the definition of its name and the teachings I have been taught by God (that I defy any theologian to dispute), means a man coming in the last days to crush the wicked — Christ the Crusher.

The Bible teaches us that means the Anointed One. But it also teaches that the Anointed One, the Christ, comes to destroy the world of evil (Christianity), a people who have taken the good name of a good prophet and put it on a religion that they teach the people; not the religion of Adam, Noah, Abraham, Moses, Jesus, and Muhammad. All of these prophets taught the same religion — that is entire submission to the Will of God. Not a new religion do the prophets bring. It has not happened so far. The basic principle of the religion of God is submission to His will.

Nimrod gets a great ovation on the 25th day of December; one of the most wicked leaders that ever lived.

He was capable of leading the white race in the last 300 years before the birth of Jesus, their last prophet.

The great false worship of December 25 is a lie. The worship of Jesus' birthday, which they claim is on the

25th of December, is one of the most open lies against the truth. And the authors of their religion, Christianity, know that they are wrong in trying to tell the world that they are wrong in trying to tell the world that that is the day Jesus was born on. Not a man on earth knows that day because it was not mentioned according to Allah, in the Person of Master Fard Muhammad, to Whom Praises are due forever, the God of the Righteous and Truth. The way that He has taught us of Jesus' history makes sense. His birth could not have been made known since the authority of his time was intended to kill him. They got a little mixed up in his appearance looking for the birth of a Mighty One to come and change the Jews' government and people for hell-fire (though Jesus, as God taught me, was actually believing that he could convert the Jews until he learned the history of the Jews). Then he changed his mind and denounced them as being a race of devils and his word of truth had no place in them, because there was no truth in them by nature. They were not made of truth; therefore, the Christmas, the 25th day of December that you worship every year, is not the birthday of Jesus.

Some of you do not care whose birthday it is just as long as you are off from work and acting like a fool, wasting up all your money that you have made that year to buy whiskey, a few fine clothes, new automobiles or something to help enrich the world that has taught you such things.

Here is what Allah taught me of the 25th day of December: He said that this is not the day that Jesus was born. Jesus was born in September between the first part of the month of September, because, as I have foresaid, the Jews were watching for his birth to kill him. But they were mistaken. The one that he was actually taken for to be Jesus was not that one. They thought that Jesus 2,000 years ago was the Mahdi, the Great Messiah that they called the Christ or the Messiah Coming at the end of their time to destroy them and set up another kingdom of the God's like Him. God taught me that the 25th day of December is the day of the birth of Nimrod, and that the scientists know that that is Nimrod's birthday.

Nimrod was a leader, born as an opponent of Moses' teachings. Allah taught me in the Person of Master Fard Muhammad, to Whom Praises are due forever, that this man was born in the last 300 years of Moses, 2,000 years. The whole of the scope of independent teachings of Moses is 1700 years and not 2,000 years. Because of this Nimrod breaks the 2,000 years by 300. But, nevertheless, Moses gets the credit for the 2,000 years, because this little fellow was not able to do what he was doing and his work was to reach not only 2,000 years, but the complete 6,000 years of the white race's civilization. Nimrod was an evil, devil man, and according to sketches of his history, here and there that you may run across as I did, nothing good is said about him. He was an opposer of Moses' Law and Order given to him from Allah (God) to guide Israel into independency of the original Nation of the earth.

The Teachings that parents give to their children of the Santa Claus coming on the night of the 24th prior to the 25th of December, to bring presents to the children, are false. And some say that his transportation is some kind of sled so he can get over the snow and ice pulled by reindeer. This is also something the children look for, as well as the children in the South, where there is hardly any snow for a cat to walk on let alone a deer. But, yet, they are taught the same thing. Then they go so far as to say that Santa Claus comes down the chimney with all those deer and with all that load of toys. Now you know that there has to be a mighty large chimney to accommodate those deer and cars of presents for the children in the community. Then the child grows up believing this is the truth as the parents affirm their lie by scratching on the back of the chimney making marks in the soot to make the child think that the Santa Claus came down the chimney. I know, as I saw and believed the same thing when I was a little boy. They had lied to me, and I thought that they were telling the truth, until I saw mommy and daddy putting things in the closet one night while I was keenly watching to see the Santa Claus. But to my suprise, it was my father and mother, and I told my sister what I had seen that night. So I was no longer a believer in the strange Santa Claus after catching them "red-handed" (slang). I could hardly enjoy the Christmas gifts that day after thinking over what I had so strongly believed what they had taught me was Santa Claus, and had learned that he was my parents. And when you learn the truth about Santa Claus after a certain age, then they stop giving you anything. They tell you that they will give you your presents in person.

Then, for the first time, the child learns the truth that he was was only deceived by what they had taught him. This teaches the child in an early stage to lie, because the parents bring him up with lying.

So I ask all the children who read this article on Santa Claus to tell your parents to give you the presents that they want to give you, and do not tell you that some Santa Claus is going to give them to you, because they are the ones who buy the presents for you. Oh yes, they take other than the truth for a lot of fun, while we cannot take other than the truth for fun, when it is not fun. That is a sin before God. There is no lie in Him at all, and if we believe and follow Him, we must be the same and not liars. But this is due to the nature of the white race who was made like that. They were a false people, leading the people wrong, falsely. And the time will come when they will wake up like the child who wakes up to the knowledge that the real Santa Claus is his father and mother. So will you wake up to the Real God for his (white race) time is up and you will find out that the God is Yourself. And your parents, the Black Man, was the first God who created the heavens and the earth.

So, my little Brother and Sister, go home and tell your parents to buy you such and such things if you want something for the 25th day of December, and tell them they can give to you as they are the ones who are the real Santa Claus for you.

And there is no such thing as your worshipping Jesus on the 25th of December. He was a righteous prophet of God, 2,000 years ago, and they disgrace this righteous prophet and his name by worshipping a false day that he was not even born on. And the material they use to worship the Jesus is drinking whisky, beer, wine, and fighting, gambling, doing all acts of evil on that day. When I was a little boy coming up, the men folk would think that they were not taking Christmas unless they had plenty of liquor and whisky to drink and they would get half drunk and vomit all over the streets and highways. It is a sin and disgrace to be calling yourself worshipping a righteous person and celebrating his birthday with all kinds of drinking and gambling. This shows you that this was not the Jesus' birthday because if you acted like this on the real birthday of the righteous, the God would punish you. You do not get away with mistreating the righteous and not be punished. The evil people have a time to flourish in evil doings to do all kinds of evil until the end of their time which is now. That evil will be punished in the day of the God of Justice and Righteousness. You will read that righteous people, even to prophets, were killed by the white race, Jews, and some of those who killed the prophets were not destroyed because it was the time that evil was to triumph over the righteous. Now, today is the day of Allah (God) and His World Will Be a World of Righteousness, Freedom, Justice, and Equality. And we cannot get away with falsehood in His Day and Time and in the building up of His Kingdom without being punished immediately.

So, I say little Brother and Sister, go home and remember that mommy and daddy are your Santa Claus, and they ride in cars and not in ice-sleds with six to eight reindeer pulling it. That number six represents the time that falsehood would triumph. That is the number of the white race, meaning they would triumph for 6,000 years.

CHAPTER 34

Days of the Son of Man:
Confusion of Nations

The prophecy of the coming of the Son of Man and the days of the Son of Man is almost the whole of the Bible, scriptures, histories and prophecies. The people who read the Bible should understand these things. You should want to read and understand.

Let us see what and who is the Son of Man who is mentioned here. We are all sons of some man, but this specifies the Son of Man coming in the Last Days to Judge man.

True understanding and the answers to these questions destroy any mistaken ideas or misunderstandings and prophecies of the Bible and Holy Qur'an concerning the coming of the Son of Man.

The true knowledge of Who is the Son of Man and Why He is Called the Son of Man destroys the teachings of the Christians concerning the prophecies of the Son of Man and the coming of the Son of Man. This forces understanding upon the world that is blind to the knowledge of Who and Why He is Called the Son of Man... especially the once slave of the white slave - masters.

The white Christians have never taught the true theology of scriptures to their Black slave; therefore they do not know Who to look for. They look for something other than a man to usher in the Judgment and Judge the world according to its sins.

The Son of Man is the Son of a Man. He is not a spirit as the ignorant are prone to believe. He is the Son of

Original Man, the Black Man.

The Bible does not each you that He is the son of mankind. Mankind is the made-man, the white man. The Great Mahdi is the Son of the Original Man, the Black Man.

The Son of mankind is the made man, the white man whom the Original Man, the Black Man, drove out of the Garden of Eden.

The Son of Man, Spoken of as Coming in the Last Days, is the Son of Original Man. Therefore they have it right when they say He is the Son of Man... that is the Original Man, the Black man.

The Great Mahdi, the God and Judge Who is now Present in the World, Master Fard Muhammad, To Whom Praises are Due forever, taught me that His Father was a real Black Man. His Father went up into the mountains (governments of the Caucasians) picking out a white woman to marry so that she would give birth to a son looking white but yet the Father is Black.

This makes the preachings of the Christians that He is a Made Man to take the burden of seeking the Lost - Found people from out of the midst of their captors who are white. He would do this work in a Day that they least expected. Therefore the Bible says he Came without observation as a thief in the night (night of Spiritual darkness) (Bible) 1 Th. 5.2.

As to the days of the Son of Man, I would rather say they refer to years rather than days consisting of twenty-four (24) hours.

The Holy Qur'an also refers to it as the 'Days' of Allah. This means 'years' as it takes years to remove a whole world and bring in a new one. There is so much that has to be done. People have to be convinced that He is Justified to remove the world of sin, for the world of sin has ruled the people for 6,000 years. There are so many people who are sold to the idea of wicked world rulers.

The Days of the Son of Man represent the Days (Years) that He Will Be Judging the world and punishing the world for her evil. The Son of Man is gathering, teaching, and training His People right in the midst of this wicked world. His People have gotten experience of the wicked world and He Teaches them how now to avoid the wicked world and its teachings and yet live in the midst of it. Their living in the midst of the evil world and yet avoiding it proves their worthiness since they have gotten experience living in the evil world and now they turn to righteousness while they are still in the midst of the evil world. These people have an experience of both evil and good. Then if these are brought out of the evil world, these people are the people that he said he Saved out of the Fire. The Holy Qur'an says that we were on a Brink of Fire.

The Son of Man... the Bible is specific in its prophecy concerning this man. It tells us that we should make no mistake for there is no other prophecy of anything other than a Man coming and judging us. We all have been preaching of the day of the Son of Man. The mistaken idea that God is a spook or spirit is due to that which was added by you and your enemy while all the time He is telling you that He is The Son of Man.

The Great Mahdi, the Saviour of His People... Bible Mt. 1:21 prophesied that He Was Born to Save His People from sin. They were guilty of the same sin as that of their evil teacher, for they practiced the same sin.

Upon the coming of God, the Son of Man, He being

184

the Just Judge of Man and man-kind, He forgave us our sins because we are not guilty of that which we did not know.

The mankind (white man) taught us from the cradle to follow after them. They separated us from our Original People of Asia and Africa in order to do a thorough job of making us other than ourselves, the Original Black Man.

The white man went in and out of our grandparents until our blood became part of theirs... so we are today. This ties us up in his blood so that it will be easy for us to practice his way of life. In order to take us out of the life and doing of the mankind people, we had to have a knowledge of them.

It is the Great Mahdi, the Great Messiah, who is so prophesied of by the Christians. Yet the Pope of Rome and his priests are trying their utmost to deceive us concerning this Great Visit of God in Person. They try to deceive us into believing that this is not yet the Day of the Son of Man. They want you to believe that they still hold the reigns on the guidance for the Black People.

This defiant act is against the manifestation of the truth of them. By the Son of Man is the reason He is punishing them. He is putting priest against priest, church against church, and Christians against the Pope of Rome as we see it today Gen. 3:15. The Bible prophesies that the serpent will bruise the heel (followers) of the woman (Messenger). This means they would deceive the followers of the Messenger. But the Messenger will bruise the head of the serpent meaning the foundation of the chief of Christianity's way of teaching.

In the Days of the Son of Man there will be much trouble and confusion of Nations. Bible Is. 2.24:1 says the whole earth will be turned upside down and nations scattered abroad. The Bible says (Mt. 25:32) "Before Him shall be gathered all nations." The Holy Qur'an says, "you shall see all nations kneeling before Him and they shall be judged out of their own books." The government keeps a record of their governmental accounts. They have books in the library and in the courts which tell how they have ruled the people. They have a record of how they have judged the people.

The Holy Qur'an says that God will Judge them out of their own books which have the condemnation of their own evil and unjust judgment which they did give out to the people, especially the poor Black slave.

Boom, that is the end when this is accomplished. When the Son of Man proves that He is Justified in destroying the wicked, then they will be destroyed in the twinkling of an eye.

CHAPTER 35

Being Ashamed of Your Own God

Because of Allah coming to us in the Person of Master Fard Muhammad, teaching us that glorious, much prophesied Truth that will put us, the Black once-slaves of white America, into heaven while we live, should we be so foolish to reject that Truth which has been brought to us to take us out of this condition of hell (subjected to white Americans); should we be ashamed to confess the Truth publicly before our ever open enemies of both the Truth and of the Black Man or deny the Name of Allah, Who Came in the Person of Master Fard Muhammad, To Whom Praises are Due forever, for the non-love and friendship of an evil people who were made by nature to hate and mistreat other Black people of the earth, we should be condemned to hell-fire along with the enemies of God.

To be ashamed to confess the God of our salvation makes us unworthy of that God's help and salvation which He has brought to us. Some of us, in the presence of white people, will deny our salvation while the white people do not, by any means, deny their hatred of the Black Man or their plans and their actions of robbery and death to the Black Man.

The white people follow the nature in which they were made, but you do not follow the nature in which you were created (righteousness and truth).

There are many Black educators, scholars, and scientists who try to keep the false friendship of white people. They dare not accept the Name of God which shall live.

Being ashamed of your own God and your own self before this evil world is like eating fire.

CHAPTER 36

Islam; A Unifying Religion

White man's Christianity has absolutely failed to get recognition and respect for us — even from those who taught it to us. It is a religion that teaches you to love your enemies and hate your friend and to seek your reward after death. It has produced more division and hate than all the other religions combined.

White Christianity has robbed and destroyed our peace and love for one another. It was white Christians who brought our fathers into slavery; it is white Christianity that is keeping you a subject people. They don't want you, nor do they like to see you go from them to your own. They fear your unity with your own.

So let us unite and be one people under the crescent of our religion, Islam. Seek for our nation what others seek for their nation; a country to ourselves where we can live in peace away from our enemies.

Islam, the religion of peace, in believing it, brings about a peace of mind and contentment. It is a unifying religion; its Author is God. It teaches against the doing of evil of every kind, great or small. The aims of Islam in America are:

1. To teach our people the truth.
2. Clean them up and make them self-respecting and unite them onto their own kind.
3. Bring them face to face with our God and teach

them to know their enemies.

The problem began 400 years ago from the very first day that our forefathers set the sole of their feet on the soil here in the Western Hemisphere in the days of John Hawkins. It was in the year 1555. Hawkins was an English slave trader. In the year 1555 when John Hawkins began bringing our people away from our own native land and away from our own people to sell us to his white brothers here in the West as merchandise for the slave markets, little did John Hawkins realize at that time that by bringing us here as slaves he was sentencing his white brothers here to their doom. For the evil that they have done and are still doing to our people here cannot be forgiven.

But it was all for a divine purpose; that Almighty God, Allah, might make Himself known, through us, to our enemies; and second, to the world that He alone is God. But our poor Black mothers and fathers, who were deceived by this devil John Hawkins and his lies and empty promises, didn't have the slightest idea that their coming here to be sold into slavery could create a problem that would take Almighty God Allah Himself and the righteous nation of Islam to solve... and that this problem would be solved at the end of the time of their archdeceiving enemies (the devils). That time has arrived. 1914 was the year. But as long as you stay asleep from lack of knowledge about yourself you are extending the life of them. They can continue to live only as long as you remain mentally dead to the knowledge of yourself and the devils.

My followers and I have spent and are still spending much time and money and are suffering much persecution and ridicule to awaken our people to the knowledge of their own salvation. But we must remember that this present suffering is nothing compared to the joy that awaits us!

Before we ever suffered ourselves, He, Master W. F. Muhammad, our God and Savior, the Great Mahdi, Almighty God Allah, in Person, suffered persecution and rejection Himself; all for you and for me.

We are now living in the days of the judgment and in the days of a great separation of peoples and nations. This problem of separating you and me from our enemies and placing us in our own land back among our own people and raising the so-called Negroes of America up to our proper place in civilization is taking place.

Remember it was Muhammad who found the black stone out of its place and invited the four chiefs from the four divisions to come forward and take hold of each corner of the mantle and lift it into its place. Remember that it was Muhammad with His own hands who guided it into its place. This was a symbol of you and me here today. We need the help of our people who are living in the four major points of our compass to come and help raise us, their dead brothers, and put us back into our own place: in our own nation among our own people in our own native land.

CHAPTER 37

Submit to Allah
(Their God)

The Divine Supreme Being. He is a Being which means that he exists and is not a spook. Christianity has blinded you to such worship as to worship that which you know not; as the Bible teaches you know not; (Bible, John 4:22). There has never been any change in the religion of Allah (God). It is this world's wickedness to deceive the Righteous that changes religion. The Pope of Rome is the father of such teachings as bringing in a religion other than the religion of Allah (God). The white race does not do the Will of our God; they were not made to do so. So do not think hard of them for not submitting to Allah (God) and for not believing in His religion, Islam. That is against their nature. However, some (few) of them here and there, throughout the world believe by faith. And now even the Pope of Rome's own preachers, priests, and cardinals are in a spirit of rebellion against Christianity because they know it is not true.

Jesus was no author of Christianity. You cannot even prove it. The Pope of Rome will not try because he is wise. He knows what Jesus taught. It was Islam, as all the prophets before him taught. And how can we get around to believing in God if we do not believe in Islam after we learn that it is entire submission to the will of God.

Submit to God. It is the nature of the Black People. God does not permit you to come to Him as His servant unless you submit to His Will, His Laws, and

His Rules. And if you are in His Country, he chases you out of it and puts you in jail for disobeying Him. This is the end of people having freedom to serve God in their own way. This is the most damnable teaching that could be taught to a man; to tell him to serve God in any way that he sees fit or to preach God's Word in the way he sees fit. This is what leads the whole entire world astray from God. Submit to the Will of Allah (The Divine Supreme Being) and see how the conditions of your life will quickly change today into better conditions.

The worst blind teaching that is going on is from Black preachers trying to prove Christianity and trying to prove that Jesus is the Son of God and that he died to save the world. This is carrying the Black Man to hell faster than anything that you can teach him; that Jesus died to save the world. This is an addition where the translators did not make it clear whose world the God will save. It was not the world of the enemies of God. This world is destined to be destroyed according to Jesus' prophecy and all the prophets before him. The Black Man does not belong to this world. The only Black Men who belong to this world are those who make themselves belong to this world. You must remember that the white man's world is a distinct world of his own. He is the god of this world until today when he meets the right Owner, The Great God, Allah. The Jesus says (Bible, John 17:9) that he did not even pray for the world; that he prayed to God to take care of those whom he had converted out of the world. He did not come to the God, praying to Him to save the world. And, again in the Bible, it is written that a sinner's prayer is not even heard. And the real sinner is the devil.

And what right do you have to preach that he died for the world when he said he did not even pray for the world or for you who are in love with the world that he was not in love with. He condemned the world as being a world of devils (Bible, John 8:44) and said that they were the prince of this world (Bible, John 12:31, Mt. 4:9). So the white race is not the universal ruler as god, but they were to rule for the time that they were given to rule. They were given power and wisdom to rule as god of their own world; and that is the civilization of the white man and his rule of the Black Man for the past 6,000 years. This means that the white race has conquered the air as well as the sea and land because they have gotten out of the rotation of the earth. This means they have conquered the atmosphere of the earth and have gone into airless space. Oh, foolish Brothers, you certainly do not know the scriptures and you are too proud to be taught. While your Bible teaches you (James 4:4) that he who loves this world is at enmity with God, the blind preachers are leading the Black People to hell as the Bible teaches; they all went in the Lake of Fire with their followers, believing in the devil (Rev. 19:20).

As Jesus was not of the world of the white man, so are we of the world of the white man. And the parable that he put before you prophesies how God would come, searching for you to take you out of the world of the wicked, and put you into your own world of Peace and security. Also see Bible (Ez. 34, Bible).

As Jesus prophesied of the Black preacher (Mt. 23:13, Bible), you will not come into the kingdom of Heaven (the religion of Islam), nor will you suffer those who are trying to come in. This is a bad scripture on the Black preacher. But you are so blind that you do not know that it is talking about you, but it is you, and not the Jews. (No. 2 Th. 2:3) says that you will not come until the man of sin was revealed.

God has raised me up among you to teach you the

194

interpretation of the Bible which you are rejecting. There is nothing in the prophecies that God has not taught me the understanding of. And if I miss telling you the Truth of the explanation that He gave to me of the Bible, I will give $10,000 for every word that you can disprove or that is not true. I am not talking about the foolish among you who want to contend and dispute on.

Read the Bible thoroughly, Black preachers and you will bear me witness that any man will be a fool to stand around and wait for the return of the Jesus who was killed here 2,000 years ago. He was nothing more than a prophet, and he has gone back to the earth, never to return alive.

As me questions or write me if you want to.

CHAPTER 38

The Cruel Days of The Lord

What causes these Days to be cruel when God Himself Is a Righteous God?

What now makes His Coming to be a Cruel Coming?

It is because He Is the Righteous God, and He is the Owner of the earth. And the previous substitute (white race), that the earth was let out to, to rule the Original Black People for a time of 6,000 years, in that time they (white race) robbed God of the worship of His People, the Original Black People.

They (white race) refused to let the people worship Allah (God). Because of the time that was left to them, instead, they made all the people, whom they could Make, to worship them (white race) as being the owner of the earth!

This angered the Real Owner! The Real Owner, Being Angry over how the non-owner had Treated the Original Black People of the earth, and how they (white race) had deceived the Original Black People, in the knowledge of the Real God and Owner—

The Real God and Owner of the earth Comes In Angry like a man who returns home and finds someone in his house who has destroyed his house and his best furniture and who has beat-up those whom the Real Owner has left among the erstwhile owner.

The Bible prophesies of the Coming of God with Anger. He is very Angry against the evil people and He is Ready to Destroy them from the face of the earth!

And everywhere there are a few who did a little good, He Does Not Destroy their Reward for a little good that they have done.

But He Comes to Destroy the wicked for the evil done to His Black People — for robbing them and killing them for nothing — only that they are the Righteous and the evil people are the wicked!

We cannot fault the wicked for doing wickedness because that is what they (white race) are made out of. They cannot do good because of the nature in which they are made!

So, the God, Being Good Himselt, by Nature — He Is Angry to Find His House torn and His People mistreated — and no one of the house offered his people any mercy — no Justice, says Isaiah, "Justice standeth afar off"—Freedom, Justice and Equality is something that they (Black People) have not known.

So, the Master, the Owner of the house (earth) is Angry. He Threatens to Destroy those who were Given rights to rule for a time!

Their time is up, so Says the Lord, and their time has been up for a long time, but they were Given a little over - time —and in the little over time that was given to them, they have not made themselves any better, they have become worse!

So it is written that "they are disagreeable to live with in peace,' which shows that regardless to how much over - time is given to them, that does not change their nature, which is to do evil, continually, against the righteous.

But, Now, Behold, His Day Have Come — the Days when He Shall Rule Himself and He Shall Deliver His Black People from such evil rule of the wicked!

CHAPTER 39

Certainty of the Punishment

(Holy Qur'an 70:6, 7,8)

Ch. 70:6, "Surely they see it far off,"

7, "And We see it nigh."

8, "The day when the heaven is as molten brass."

The Holy Qur'an, is the truest religious Book, that can be found on the planet earth. It gives guidance to the wisest philosopher and to the most ignorant savage says Maulana Muhammad Ali, (translator of the Holy Qur'an out of the Arabic language into the English language). It is a wonderful Book. It verifies the truth of the Bible. Most of the teachings of the Holy Qur'an are directed to the Last Messenger, Muhammad. It is to inform him and teach him the truth of the Resurrection of the mentally dead whom he is commissioned to Raise.

The Resurrection of his people is the Judgment of both the righteous and the wicked. The Holy Qur'an is mostly directed to the American so-called Negro, the Lost-Found Members of their Nation. It is to acquaint them with the knowledge of the immediate Judgment and with the enemy of the righteous.

The Black Man must have a thorough knowledge of the enemy (devil) and a thorough knowledge of self; for by no means can they be directed rightly until they have a thorough knowledge of self and the devil and a thorough knowledge of Allah (God)

The Lost-Found Black People, being reared by the devil; the devil knows them while they do not know him. Therefore, the Holy Qur'an was given and taught to Muhammad for the express purpose of saving his people from the fire of hell.

It is so strange now today to see that the Black Man of America desires not to be separated from his enemy, but desires that the enemy and himself live together in love of each other, as brothers, while the enemy knows that it cannot be done. But he can use their ignorant love and belief in him to take him to hell with him.

Therefore, Allah (God) has to Strike both parties, the white man (devil) and the Black, blind, deaf and dumb lovers of their enemy, with a severe chastisement, in order to open their blind eyes, as he did in Jesus' parable of the rich man and the poor man, Lazarus (Bible Luke 16:19-25). Lazarus refused to give up begging his master for survival until Allah (God) sent a famine on the rich man. The worse famine that man has ever seen is prophecied to come upon America.

CHAPTER 40

The Angry World

The rapid spread of evil over the people is a manifestation of what is in the world that is called Christianity. The Great spread of both evil and filth is staggering in the Eyes of Allah (God) and the righteous.

The Holy Qur'an teaches us to "fear a day where evil is spreading far and wide."

The resurrection of the mentally dead Black People brings about the anger of those (white man) who put the Black Man to mental death. Both people are angry; the Black slave and the slavemaster. The lack of justice to the Black slave is the cause of this anger.

Allah (God) Himself is bringing these things to pass because it is time that the mentally dead, so-called Negro and the Black People all over the earth should rise. The customary rule throughout history has been that the Black Man is the victim and he has been exploited most by all civilizations.

The Black man is the true owner of the earth. Now the God of Justice Has Risen up to Deliver the rule back to the Black Man and give him a place in the sun that justifies his ownership.

The Black Man of America (so-called Negro) did not know that he had fallen from such a high place until the Coming of Allah (God), in the Person of Master Fard Muhammad, to Whom Praises are due forever. Allah (God) taught me the history of both people: the Black and the white. He has given me the truth, wherein you see that it is being made manifest. You cannot get out of it because it is liken unto the light of the sun. We cannot get out of the light of the sun. When the sun shines on us, it banishes darkness...so it is with the truth. When the truth is told, it condemns falsehood and banishes it.

The Black man has been ruled under falsehood by a false teacher (devil). His teachings are false because he did not teach the people truth. The devil himself, was not made out of truth; he was made out of falsehood (Bible Jn. 8:44). Therefore, the Black People who follow the white man (their made enemy) are not following truth; they are following falsehood.

The religion of the white man (Christianity) is falsehood. The white man adds falsehood to the truth and mixes truth with falsehood. Formerly this blinded the eyes of the man who had lost the knowledge of himself (Black man of America).

The white man is now angry because Allah (God) Has Brought you and me the truth. They are despairing in their work of trying to get you to disbelieve the truth. The truth is your salvation and their damnation. They will put forth every effort to keep you from paying attention to the truth which has come to you.

Yes, the white man will offer you plenty of wealth as they are offering the invitation for you to walk into their homes and mix with their families by intermarrying with them.

They know that in the days of your ignorance, you admired them and that you always wanted to intermarry with them. They know this of you Now they throw the door wide open, giving you this freedom at a time when it will take you to hell if you intermarry with them. Think about what you are

201

marrying. Allah (God) has uncovered them.

Certainly they hate me for teaching you. Certainly they hated all the Messengers of God (Prophets) (Iki. 19:10). The Bible teaches you their history and tells of the denunciation of them from being the killers of the Prophets of God and we see this made manifest today in my work among you.

The white man is always planning my death because they hate the truth. The truth makes manifest their evil deeds, against you. They are angry and therefore the spreading of evil is from the angry people of Christian-doom.

The devil (white man) will deceive many of you (Bible Rev. 12:9) with his soft buttered words and his love songs and with his promises to you that he never intends to fulfill (Holy Qur'an 4:120). It is written of him that he will deceive you in this way. But by having a thorough knowledge of the archdeceiver, you should not fall victim of his deceitful teaching and love - making. Any sane man who knows fire and its burn is not going to put his hand in it. So when you know these things a surety, with experience, you should not be partakers of it.

Black People...Black men and women of intelligence and decency cannot walk the streets day or night without being tormented with the evil and filth that is practiced around them. The evildoers have no respect of decency. Robbery and murder are the order of the day here in Christian-doom. Children murder children. Children are robbing like grown-ups. No one can trust the other in such evil time.

America is the modern Sodom and Gomorrah. "Fear the day when evil is spreading far and wide."

CHAPTER 41

The Two Worlds, The Two Camps

The World is divided into two camps—Islam and Christianity. Christianity, or we may say, the white man, has been in power for 6,000 years. He has ruled independently since the birth of Moses, 4,000 years.

Islam came to Israel from Moses. Israel rebelled and Nimrod broke the civilization of Moses in the 17th century from Moses. So Allah (God) Who Came in the Person of Master Fard Muhammad, To Whom Praises are due forever, taught me.

Confusion, dissatisfaction, rebelling, fighting, and warring have ever been in Israel's and Christianity's camp due to their desire to follow the very nature in which they were made... making mischief in the land and causing bloodshed.

The time of the camp of Islam has arrived. Islam desires to take over. She will take over. Islam will rule the people under and in a government of Peace, Freedom, Justice, and Equality.

This is angering the old world of rebelling and warring against each other... Judaism and Christianity.

The two camps are angry with each other, but the anger of Islam is slow to come to its boiling point, as is cool water. In order to bring cool water to its boiling point, it is necessary to subject it to a heat of 212 degrees Fahrenheit. But spirits, chemicals, are easy to bring to a boil. They will boil at point approximately 170 degrees Fahrenheit.

These two boiling points of water and spirits can

easily be classified as the very nature of Islam and Christianity. These two worlds are now boiling over with dissatisfaction and anger against each other.

Christianity now seeks peace but she is guilty of making trouble and of starting the woes that the people now suffer. She seeks peace and seems not to be able to find it. She runs to and fro, to nations, capitols of nations, leaders and rulers, seeking peace, but finds none, it is clear, as it is written, Bible, Eze. 7:25.

The Beast, Bible, Rev. 13:2 is the symbolic name of the ruler of the United States of America. It is a very bad and ugly name, but it is the truth, and very understandable, as we see it today. The dragon gives the beast power. Here recently, we have two presidents of the United States of America who have left the seat of authority and have flown to the Vatican City of Rome to have an audience with the Pope of Rome in the hour of most needed advice.

The Pope of Rome is the god of Christianity and not Jesus. The Pope rules the Christian world as a father rules his family. He is represented by some of the theologians in Christianity as being the Vice-General of God. But the prophets see him as far from being the Vice-General of God; otherwise they would not have given him the name, "dragon."

We cannot deny the fact that these references are made in regard to the head of a government and not the beast or animal of the forest.

These two camps, Islam and Christianity, are clashing at intervals and on small scales. One writer of scriptures, in his prophecy of the final clash between the two camps (two religions), says that when Islam and Christianity meet on the battlefield for a show-down, it will be the end of the cross. The theologians and scientists of Christianity know this very well.

That which is written of the two camps (two religions): the scriptures must be fulfilled.

The God of Freedom, Justice, and Equality desires to take over in His time, and not before. This is His Time to remove the burden of suffering and mistreatment under the law of their own courts from the shoulders of the people.

He desires to set up a government without this type of court (christian) which claims to be the courts of justice, but on examining their decisions, we find that the christian courts are courts of injustice.

America is in a perilous condition. Why? Because she will not yield to the acceptance of the truth and the doing of justice to those to whom she can do justice, if she will, (her Black slave).

This is the real reason we are in this condition of seeking Justice and Peace; because the American government will not give her Black slaves Justice, nor will she allow or help them to go for themselves. She will not do that. She may be forced to do it, but she is not going to do it willingly. Because of this, The God of Freedom, Justice, and Equality is angry and so is the Nation of Islam, the Nation of Peace.

Knowing their mentality, America now sets out to deceive her once slaves, and now free-slaves who number between 20-30 million with a meaningless offer of social equality but never any earth to live on.

Allah (God) is well able to take the kingdom from whom He Pleases and give it to whom He Pleases ...this we all know. America should, as it is written, give up the slave and set him on the road to doing something for himself in the way of financing him to do this.

America is spending billions of dollars in a futile attempt to stop the stormy war clouds that are hovering over her concessions but she is not getting at the root cause of it. The reason why the cloud is rising with destruction is because of her so-called Negro slaves whom she refuses to let go.

She divides them one against the other for her own sake. It has not proven worthwhile. It has proven to be against her own peace because the God of the so-called Negro is on the scene and is Directing His Own Cause, as it is written, Bible, Is. 43:13.

Again the Bible teaches us, Is. 59:14... "...and justice standeth afar off: for truth is fallen in the street." This is true of America, and yet she looks for peace. How can she find peace when she is guilty of breaking the peace of the world and refusing to let her prisoners (so-called Negroes) go Is. 14:17.

The so - called Negro is too wild. He does not know how to strike to obtain the result of Justice for himself. He is swinging wildly, but still the God is with him to bring to pass that which is written.

I say to you, my Black brothers and sisters throughout America, join onto Islam. Follow me and I will lead you into the right way and God will bless you with that which you desire in your heart of good.

CHAPTER 42

The Threatened Day

As the Heavens are full of stars, it does not seem possible to the naked eye that we need add any more stars because the heavens are full of stars.

As the Heavens are full of stars, so it is with the population of the earth today. The population of the earth is the greatest that it has been for the past 6,000 years under the rule of the white race.

On our planet earth, every race in every country, city, and town is now so full of people that they have to look for room for expansion.

It is an acute situation throughout the earth. Governments are taxed to the limit to try to house their population.

This known, well-visited earth, in spite of its liberal habitations, is seemingly over populated, so much so that it is a problem of the governments to find houses for its citizens.

Allah Himself threatens to reduce the seemingly over population of the earth by removing all of the people of the planet earth who are unwilling to submit in obedience of Allah (God), His Messenger, and the Message that he has sent.

A great vacancy would be left, for there is only a small percentage of the population of the earth who want to do righteousness.

Much of the population of the earth has its own god and religion. They will not let go of what they have for Allah (God) and His True Religion, Islam.

My Black Brothers and Sisters, I am sorry for you if

you think that the white man's religion of Christianity will take you to heaven. I am sorry to tell you that it will not.

The Holy Qur'an teaches us that if we bring any other religion, other than Islam, on that Day, it will not be accepted. Allah (God) forbids us to set up a god beside Him, making another His Equal. The Bible teaches you the same.

You have disobeyed and added gods to the One God (Allah). The belief of the believer in Christianity is in three gods. This is against the teachings of Allah (God), The One God.

I am your God, warns Allah (God), I and I Alone. But you have set up some other I's with Allah, The One God. Allah (God) warned all prophets of the past, "Tell the people, do not set up any other god with me as My Equal. I Am Your God."

The true religion, Islam, is the Beginning of God Himself. That is the age of Islam. The age of Christianity is only 2,000 years. It's impossible to reconcile Christianity as being the true religion of God with a few words of christianity used as proof.

You are the losers...those of you who hold on to the religion of Christianity. This is the threatened day against you. You want to put aside Allah (God) and His True Religion, Islam, His Messenger and His Message, and accept that which you hope to put in its place, Christianity. This will not be accepted by Allah (God).

The heavens are full of stars. Maulana Muhammad Ali's translation of the Holy Qur'an, in his footnote in that Chapter, says this represents a prosperous people and behind this prosperous people is a threatened destruction. They are in high places and authority of the earth.

The enemies of Allah (God) are working to reduce the population of the Planet Earth by means of poisoning the human beings and by setting up birth control laws under very wicked devices in order to rid the earth of people according to their idea of controlling the increase of the races and nations of the earth. This is a wicked thing.

Few people recognize the fact that we are living in the Day of Judgment of the wicked. You would like to ignore it. Why? It is because they love this wicked world which the wicked have built. They do not want to depart from it.

Allah (God) has given me the truth for the people. But in every city and town, and on every street, little would-be leaders snatch a few words of what Allah (God) has given to me for you, and they try to build an independent organization for self. Not for you...but for themselves.

REBELLIOUS LEADERSHIP

This independent leadership is for self-exaltation. It is written in both the Bible and the Holy Qur'an that all want to be their own leader, all want to be shepherds of the people. They want honor for themselves regardless of Allah's (God's) warning to them to follow His Shepherd Whom He has Chosen...me. They depend upon themselves and they have nothing and they will never be successful. I do not worry about these little self-guides, self-leaders and self-organizations:

I warn the public. You are headed to be burned if you follow these self-styled leaders. You may say to me, Muhammad, we think you are self-styled. I say to you, calculate on my work. Allah (God) is with me to enable me to do it. If you do not believe that He Is, I still say, you should follow a man who is doing what I am doing since you are not able to do it.

Stop splitting up the Black people throughout America and setting up opposition to the work which Allah (God) has appointed for me to do which is the salvation of the Black People and your salvation.

This sitting around waiting to see will get you hell like it did the people of Noah, Lot, and Pharaoh. The Holy Qur'an warns you against this, "Wait if want to. We too are waiting." It gives a very stern theological answer, "We know that you are on the wrong base. The Bible teaches you of the Muslims: "We know what we worship, you worship ye know not what."

You are so far from understanding the prophecies of Jesus...making him something coming back from the grave in the Judgment to Judge the people with God. The Bible plainly tells you that he died "I go away..." then he prophesied that "God will send you one." You do not want that to be the present Messenger of Allah (God) whom you are opposed to. But you keep trying to preach the dead prophet, Jesus, back to life. Jesus was nothing but a prophet and he did not deny it. I have contended with you on this.

Let the Pope of Rome contend with me, for you are not able to attempt to do so. You are blind to the theology of Christianity. You do not have enough knowledge of theology and scripture to contend with me.

The white man would not teach you the right understanding of the scripture of the Bible. Many times, I have invited any one of them to prove the claim that the Jesus of 2,000 years ago is coming back.

We know what happened to him 2,000 years ago. He cannot come back from the grave. He is not in heaven. This is a lack of knowledge of the theology of the scriptures, but you can believe it any way that you want to. I would not give you 2¢ for all your praying to a dead Jesus to hear you. He does not hear you. He is dead and buried as all others before him and since who have died.

WORLD-WIDE MISSION

You 'little leaders you think that because few ignorant people follow you you think that you have advantage with the people.

Allah (God) Who Came in the Person of Master Fard Muhammad, To Whom Praises are due forever, is Independent and I, His Messenger, am an independent, Proud, Black Man. There are millions of people on this earth besides you. I can teach them in six (6) hours and they will believe more than you do in six (6) years of my teaching you.

Allah (God) will whip you into submission. That is what He Will Do...The Heavens are Full Of Stars...The Threatened Day.

CHAPTER 43

Old World Going Out;
New World Come In

The Old World of mischiefmaking and bloodshed is now on its way out in order make room for the new world of Righteousness and Peace.

For the past 6,000 years we have had to live in an evil world that was designed to destroy the peace of man and to shed his blood.

All around the earth, there has not been one section of the world in which the Original Man has been or where he now lives that has not been touched or ruled by the evil of gods of the old world.

The God of Righteousness and peace, today, has Made His Appearance to Take to Himself the Rule of the Nations under the government of Peace, Freedom, Justice, and Equality.

Allah (God) Seeks to separate the evil from the good and the good from the evil. He Declared Himself as Coming to Seek and to Save the Black Man (so-called Negro) from his kidnappers (the white race).

Allah (God) Came to unite and Restore the Black Man again to his Own and Bless Him with the rule of the Nations of earth, as declared by the prophets, Abraham, Moses, and Jesus.

Fall of Ancient Babylon

In The Fall of Ancient Babylon Jer. 50:46, "At the noise of the taking of Babylon the earth is moved, and the cry is heard among the nations." here the Bible teaches us and we see today, at the fall of the old

212

world, there is a great noise of war, the fighting of war, the destruction of nations, towns, and cities and the killing of their citizens. There is disagreement and confusion of the heads of nations.

It is a very dreadful time that the populations of the earth are now living in. This is the time of the destruction of a world. It is not to be compared with the destruction of an organization or a few towns as it was in the days of Noah. The destruction today is the destruction of a whole world. The prophets could not have given us a better picture of what we may expect today than the picture of what took place in the fall of ancient Babylon.

The Earth, land, and sea are set in battle array. Every type of deadly weapon is fashioned and is now being used against man and man. See Holy Qur'an Chap. 30:41. There cannot be any peace for man under these conditions.

CHAPTER 44

The Great Day

We are living in a Great Day of God and Man. Allah (God) now Desires to take for Himself to Reign over the nations of the earth.

There are two Gods. One god is the god of the evil and the Other is the God of Righteousness and Justice. The nature of the two Gods is so much different from the other that it makes it impossible for one God to yield to the other God because of their nature.

Unrighteousness and injustice have triumphed over the people for the past six thousand (6,000) years. The unjust god was not one to give up his place for the God of Justice. Well, we cannot blame him since by nature he was made a god; a ruler. But his time is out and his rule is up. He is now in the time of the other God — the God of Righteousness, Freedom, Justice, and Equality.

So this is a Great Day — the passing away of one world and the coming in of another world. We have suffered under the evil that the devil was made for. Up until this very minute he wants to do all the evil that he can do regardless to the Bible and the Holy Qur'an teaching that Allah (God) Will Reward him and me for every good act or good work.

Everything is being changed from the old to a new thing.

We Must Qualify For The New.

CHAPTER 45

Revelation Guide All Right

Holy Qur'an Chapter 42: 46-49

46 And they will have no friends to help them beside Allah. And he whom Allah leaves in error cannot find a way.

47 Hearken to your Lord before there comes from Allah the day which there is no averting. You will have no refuge on that day, nor will it be yours to make a denial.

48 But if they turn away, We have not sent thee as a watcher over them. Thy duty is only to deliver (the message). And surely when we make man taste mercy from us, he rejoices thereat; and if as evil afflicts them on account of what their hands have sent before, then surely man is ungrateful.

49. Allah's is the kingdom of the heavens and the earth. He creates what He pleases. He grants females to whom He pleases and grants males to whom He pleases.

The above four verses of the 42nd Chapter of the Holy Qur'an warns a disbeliever and a hypocrite that on that Day of the Resurrection and Judgment of this world, our people will not find a friend to help them besides Allah (God) Who Came in the Person of Master Fard Muhammad to Whom praises are due forever. It also warns us that if we do not accept Him, if we are in an error, He will leave us in that error and we cannot benefit with right guidance from ourselves.

This right guidance must come from Allah through a Messenger that He sends to you in the time of the

Resurrection and Judgment of the world who has a heart and mind like God's Himself; the executor of the wicked. This Messenger that He has in that day and time will only love and do that which God Himself loves and does. And the 47th verse says that you should hear the teachings of the truth in the words that it gives you before that day comes. For in that time, you cannot get extra time to think it over. You must think it over before that day comes. The 47th verse warns us thoroughly that on that day, we will have no way of seeking refuge from the evil destruction of that day.... only with God alone (in the Person of Master Fard Muhammad). And you will not have the power on that day to make a denial.

Verse 48 clears the Messenger of the people going astray after hearing this Truth, ignoring it, and not accepting it, by telling him that he was not set as a watcher over them to see whether they did right or wrong. He was only to deliver the message. He was not to set around and watch and see if they did right; that is up to them. And He Does Not Punish us; only according to that which we do of evil with knowledge of that thing.

Verse 49 teaches us that the Kingdom is Allah's...the heavens and the earth. And, this is true as I teach you plainly from His Mouth, that the heavens and the earth belong to the Black Man and what is in them and what comes out of them and comes down to them, it all belongs to Allah, The Black Nation. So let us fly to Allah before we are forced to do it, and then get turned down.

Truth Shall Be Established
Holy Qur'an Chapter 57:20 & 22
20 Know that this world's life is only sport and play gaiety and boasting among yourselves and a vying in

the multiplication of wealth and children. It is as rain, whose causing the vegetation to grow please the husbandmen, then it withers away so that thou seest it turning yellow, then it becomes chaff. And in the Hereafter is a severe chastisement, and (also) forgiveness from Allah and (His) pleasure. And this world's life is naught but a source of vanity.

22 No disaster befalls in the earth, or in yourselves, but it is in a book before We bring it into existence—surely that is easy to Allah—

Commentary

This is a sign of how the people are now...that after the world (of the wicked) seemingly has been successful with wasting their time in sport and play, it is classified as vegetation when it is getting rain on it and it grows and flourishes. But when the rain ceases to come, and the vegetation is exposed to sun's heat, it withers away. So it is with the wicked after living a life of wickedness and carelessness and wasting his time in sport and play. Then the time of truth comes demanding him not to waste him time in sport and play but to do service to Allah and to self...for the Holy Qur'an teaches us again and again that the heavens and the earth were not made for sport and play.

You notice that our Black People...especially here in America...have become sold to nothing in the world but sport and play. This is the way the people were of Lot and Noah; they were sold to sport and play and they hated the teachings of those righteous Prophets. And the day of their doom came, unexpected to them because they did not heed their warnings. So it is here today...24 hours a day...they are trying to have sport and play and talking over foolish things, spending their time in foolishness. I fear of an evil day overtaking my people here in America soon.

True.... the world is warning you now, and you act as though the white people can help it. But they are telling you now that unemployment keeps mounting and they can do nothing about it. They are warning you that you are going to get hungry too, but you are not trying to take it with sincerity that they are telling you the truth. You are like a child who cries to its mother for bread and milk, whether there is any in the kitchen or not.

So this is you... a big, old, grown child, who has been nursed and fed by the white people and sheltered by them and you think you will always have this from them. But No Sir...remember the parable of Lazarus and the rich man. At last, the rich man died and in his death of poverty, he came to suffer the same thing that Lazarus suffered...being deprived of good homes, and luxury of all kinds. This will be taken in this day and time. But the righteous will flourish with whatever they please with God.

Study the Holy Qur'an; it is full of wisdom.

INDEX

INDEX

221

INDEX

The
Muslim Program
What the Muslims Believe

1.   WE BELIEVE in the One God Whose proper Name is Allah.

2.   WE BELIEVE in the Holy Qur'an and in the Scriptures of all the Prophets of God.

3.   WE BELIEVE in the truth of the Bible but we believe that it has been tampered with and must be reinterpreted so that mankind will not be snared by the falsehoods that have been added to it.

4.   WE BELIEVE in Allah's Prophets and the Scriptures they brought to the people.

5.   WE BELIEVE in the resurrection of the dead—not in physical resurrection—but in mental resurrection. We believe that the so-called Negroes are most in need of mental resurrection: therefore, they will be resurrected first.

Furthermore, we believe we are the people of God's choice, as it has been written, that God would choose the rejected and the despised. We can find no other persons fitting this description in these last days more than the so-called Negroes in America. We believe in the resurrection of the righteous.

6.   WE BELIEVE in the judgment; we believe this first judgment will take place as God revealed, in America...

7.   WE BELIEVE this is the time in history for the separation of the so-called Negroes and the so-called white Americans. We believe the black man should be freed in name as well as in fact. By this we mean that he should be freed from the names imposed upon him by his former slave masters. Names which identified him as being the slave master's slave. We believe that if we are free indeed, we should go in our own people's names—the black peoples of the earth.

8.   WE BELIEVE in justice for all, whether in God or not; we believe as others, that we are due equal justice as human beings. We believe in equality—as a nation—of equals. We do not believe that we are equal with our slave masters in the status of "freed slaves."

Continued:

What the Muslims Believe

We recognize and respect American citizens as independent peoples and we respect their laws which govern this nation.

9. WE BELIEVE that the offer of integration is hypocritical and is made by those who are trying to deceive the black peoples into believing that their 400-year-old enemies of freedom, justice and equality are, all of a sudden, their "friends." Furthermore, we believe that such deception is intended to prevent black people from realizing that the time in history has arrived for the separation from the whites of this nation.

If the white people are truthful about their professed friendship toward the so-called Negro, they can prove it by dividing up America with their slaves.

We do not believe that America will ever be able to furnish enough jobs for her own millions of unemployed, in addition to jobs for the 20,000,000 black people as well.

10. WE BELIEVE that we who declared ourselves to be righteous Muslims, should not participate in wars which take the lives of humans. We do not believe this nation should force us to take part in such wars, for we have nothing to gain from it unless America agrees to give us the necessary territory wherein we may have something to fight for.

11. WE BELIEVE our women should be respected and protected as the women of other nationalities are respected and protected.

12. WE BELIEVE that Allah (God) appeared in the Person of Master W. Fard Muhammad, July, 1930; the long-awaited "Messiah" of the Christians and the "Mahdi" of the Muslims.

We believe further and lastly that Allah is God and besides HIM there is no God and He will bring about a universal government of peace wherein we all can live in peace together.

224

What the Muslims Want

This is the question asked most frequently by both the whites and the blacks. The answers to this question I shall state as simply as possible.

1. We want freedom. We want a full and compete freedom.

2. We want justice. Equal justice under the law. We want justice applied equally to all, regardless of creed or class or color.

3. We want equality of opportunity. We want equal membership in society with the best in civilized society.

4. We want our people in America whose parents or grandparents were descendants from slaves, to be allowed to establish a separate state or territory of their own—either on this continent or elsewhere. We believe that our former slave masters are obligated to provide such land and that the area must be fertile and minerally rich. We believe that our former slave masters are obligated to maintain and supply our needs in this separate territory for the next 20 to 25 years—until we are able to produce and supply our own needs.

Since we cannot get along with them in peace and equality, after giving them 400 years of our sweat and blood and receiving in return some of the worst treatment human beings have ever experienced, we believe our contributions to this land and the suffering forced upon us by white America, justifies our demand for complete separation in a state or territory of our own.

5. We want freedom for all Believers of Islam now held in federal prisons. We want freedom for all black men and women now under death sentence in innumerable prisons in the North as well as the South.

We want every black man and woman to have the freedom to accept or reject being separated from the slave master's children and establish a land of their own.

We know that the above plan for the solution of the black and white conflict is the best and only answer to the problem between two people.

6. We want an immediate end to the police brutality and mob attacks against the so-called Negro throughout the United States.

We believe that the Federal government should intercede to see that

225

What the Muslims Want

black men and women tried in white courts receive justice in accordance with the laws of the land—or allow us to build a new nation for ourselves, dedicated to justice, freedom and liberty.

7.   As long as we are not allowed to establish a state or territory of our own, we demand not only equal justice under the laws of the United States, but equal employment opportunities—now!

We do not believe that after 400 years of free or nearly free labor, sweat and blood, which has helped America become rich and powerful, that so many thousands of black people should have to subsist on relief, charity or live in poor houses.

8.   We want the government of the United States to exempt our people from ALL taxation as long as we are deprived of equal justice under the laws of the land.

9.   We want equal education—but separate schools up to 16 for boys and 18 for girls on the condition that the girls be sent to women's colleges and universities. We want all black children educated, taught and trained by their own teachers.

Under such schooling system we believe we will make a better nation of people. The United States government should provide, free, all necessary text books and equipment, schools and college buildings. The Muslim teachers shall be left free to teach and train their people in the way of righteousness, decency and self respect.

10.   We believe that intermarriage or race mixing should be prohibited. We want the religion of Islam taught without hinderance or suppression.

These are some of the things that we, the Muslims, want for our people in North America.

226

Made in United States
Orlando, FL
26 February 2023

30400902R00127